BLACK BELT.
B·O·O·K·S

The Beginner's Guide to the
LONG SWORD

European Martial Arts Weaponry Techniques

Steaphen Fick

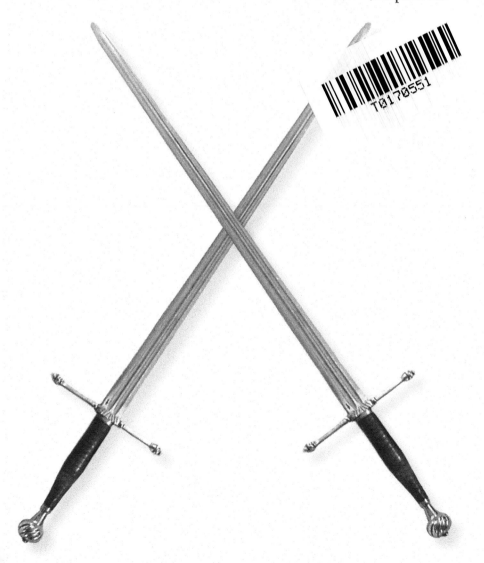

The Beginner's Guide to the
LONG SWORD
European Martial Arts Weaponry Techniques

Steaphen Fick

Edited by Sarah Dzida, Raymond Horwitz, Jeannine Santiago
and Jon Sattler

Graphic Design by John Bodine

Model: Brian Stewart

Photography by Michael Morgan

©2009 Black Belt Communications LLC
All Rights Reserved
Printed in the United States of America
Library of Congress Control Number: 2009903963
ISBN-10: 0-89750-178-0
ISBN-13: 978-0-89750-178-1

Second Printing 2013

BLACK BELT BOOKS
A Division of **OHARA** ⫿ **PUBLICATIONS, INC.**
World Leader in Martial Arts Publications

Acknowledgments

I want to thank all my friends and fellow sword practitioners for helping me put this book together. Whenever I work with fellow practitioners of the European martial arts, I learn something new that helps me grow and improve as a swordsman. The desire to master the theories and applications of swordplay creates the perfect environment of camaraderie to safely study this art. The opportunity to perfect myself as a swordsman is what makes me look forward to each and every step of the path that I have chosen. Meeting others that have chosen to travel this path is one of the greatest pleasures that I have in my life.

Of all the people who I have met on my path, the two greatest are John Hudson and Ivor Burge. John has been practicing and teaching modern fencing for 45 years, and Ivor researched and practiced historic forms of the European arts for more than seven years. John and I have had some great discussions about every aspect of the sword and the art of using it. Ivor lived in Japan for many years where he studied the art of Japanese swordsmanship. Ivor was a great friend and one of the first people to see me as a teacher—he made me believe that I possessed knowledge about this noble art that I could pass on to others.

While there are many other people that I would like to acknowledge, I will have to stop with these two great traveling companions on this 1,000-mile trek I am on.

Preface

The process of studying any martial art is like a path. This path is a 1,000-mile trek, and this book is meant to be the first step on that path for people who have an interest, even a passing one, in sword fighting.

The book focuses on the long sword for two reasons. The first reason is purely selfish: The long sword is my first love. The second reason is that because the long sword is larger, its movements are bigger and easier to illustrate in a book. Also, when people think of a "sword," movies like *Conan the Barbarian*, *The Lord of the Rings* and *Camelot* or video games like World of Warcraft, EverQuest or Soul Calibur come to mind. Simply put, the long sword is what is commonly associated with sword fighting.

Along with my own experiences from fighting in armor at tournaments and Renaissance faires for over two decades, I'll also refer to the teachings of Italian sword master Fiore dei Liberi in his treatise *Fior di Battaglia* (Flower of Battle), which was first presented in 1409. Dei Liberi was 70 years old when he wrote the book, which is based on what he learned while fighting in wars, tournaments and duels. Many of his lessons are valid today and I tend to fight and teach in the Italian style anyway.

If you want to continue your long-sword training, my book will give you a good starting place for your path of study. Otherwise, this book is a beginner's guide for people who've always wanted to learn something about the sword but didn't know where to begin, readers who are content to study the long sword from their couches, or enthusiasts who plan to break out their lightsabers.

No matter your background or skill level, this book is for you. Enjoy!

—Steaphen Fick
2009

Table of Contents

Introduction

While most of us have picked up a stick at some point in our lives to pretend that we're sword fighting, others are forging a renaissance for the European martial arts. Moviemakers, game designers, authors, martial arts instructors and club organizers are rediscovering sword fighting and showcasing various sword styles. Because of this, it's safe to say that the European martial arts are more popular now than they've ever been since the 1800s.

Generally, most people are familiar with modern sword fencing as a sport, like in the Olympics or in movies like *Highlander* and *Robin Hood*. What some people don't appreciate is that the sport originally came from the martial art of sword fighting. The art includes many dimensions like physics, geometry, self-confidence and personal self-defense. It also includes techniques for the battlefield or dueling with classic weapons such as the rapier, side sword or long sword.

The rapier is a single-handed, double-edged, long thrusting sword used from the late 16th century through the end of the 17th century. It has a compound hilt (a protective cage over the hand) and is commonly associated with great fictional swordsmen like The Three Musketeers and Zorro.

rapier

Photos by Steaphen Fick

The side sword was popular in the 16th century and is a cross between the long sword and rapier. The side sword was designed much like the rapier. It is a single-handed, double-edged sword with a compound hilt and a wide blade for cutting. Hollywood has used this type of sword in *The Mask of Zorro*, *The Revenge of Zorro* and *The Chronicles of Narnia: Prince Caspian*.

side sword

The long sword—used between the 14th and 17th centuries—is most commonly associated with knights and is used in movies like *The Lord of the Rings, Monty Python and the Holy Grail,* and *Black Knight.* This book focuses solely on the guards, techniques and principles of the long sword. Because of its size, the long sword's movements are easier to depict in pictures, but the sword fundamentals in this beginner's guide are universal.

long sword

The book is divided into three parts. Section I discusses universal sword concepts that apply to the long sword. Section II and Section III expand on drills that you can safely practice with your friends or fellow students. Like any martial art, sword training requires constant practice so that the moves and techniques become ingrained into your memory. This "muscle memory" allows you to adapt in any fighting situation. While it's unlikely that you'll have to worry about being attacked by a sword-wielding maniac, constant practice does build self-confidence and a greater awareness of everyday life.

Even the simplest drill in this book will seem awkward at first. Remembering how to hold the sword, defending your openings, moving your feet correctly and staying on target will seem overwhelming. Eventually, it will be like riding a bike: Your body will know implicitly what to do to support your actions.

I've also organized this book to accommodate many different kinds of readers—those who are hoping to learn about the long sword for fun, for educational purposes or as a jumping-off point to training with an instructor. If you're just here to understand sword fighting in movies or recognize movement in live-action role-play games, this book is still for you. But for those of you who are looking for a path to true mastery, this book will assist you with that process and help you begin your journey as a true student of the sword. It will also be a useful reference for you on this 1,000-mile trek.

So let's begin.

Section I

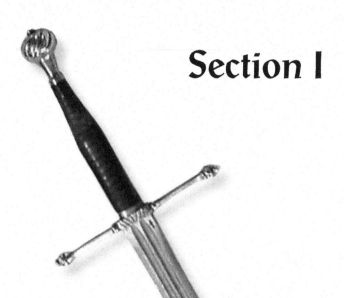

In the Beginning, There Was Theory

Note to Reader:

This first section is an introduction to the long sword. You do not need to have a sword or object in your hands to understand the material within; instead, just sit back and relax. Even though this section has no drills, it offers a foundation for the later sections.

Chapter 1:
Parts of the Sword

The sword we discuss in this book is the long sword, which is also known as the hand-and-a-half sword, great sword or bastard sword. The long sword is sometimes called the hand-and-a-half sword because it is light enough to swing with one hand, but you can grip the hilt with both hands for more powerful strikes. It's sometimes called the great sword or, as it was known in the 15th century, the great war sword because it was a large military weapon. (Note: *Claymore* means great sword in Gaelic, which is the long sword!). And it's sometimes called the bastard sword because it is longer than a single-handed sword but shorter than a two-handed sword. You might come across these different names while reading books, watching movies or playing games. The long sword is just the most common of them all.

Many people wrongly believe that the blade is the only useful part of the sword. Movies, novels and video games have reinforced this misconception by showing heroes who only use the sword for cutting and stabbing. In reality, every part of the sword from the pommel to the point is a weapon that can be used for attack and defense. Depending on what part of the sword you are using, the long sword is actually three different weapons. If you hold the handle, you have a sword. If you have one hand on the handle and one hand on the blade, then you turn your sword into a dagger. If you hold both hands on the blade, you turn your sword into hammer.

In this book, you will learn how to use the sword when held by the handle and when the blade is used for cutting. To understand how the different techniques work and why, it is important to know the names for all the sword parts because I will be referring to them throughout this book.

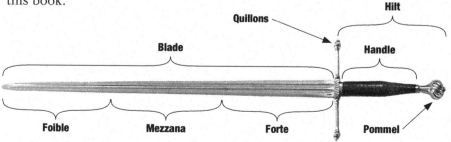

The Pommel

Have you ever heard of the phrase "pummeling someone into submission"? This common English idiom takes its origins from the sword pommel. The pommel is the counterweight at the end of the sword handle, and it helps balance the weight of the blade, making it easier to use and move around. In combat, the pommel could also be used to strike an adversary at distances that are too close for the blade. Filippo Vadi wrote a treatise on sword fighting in 1482 called *Arte Gladiatoria*. In it, he uses the phrase "hammer his mustache" to refer to a face strike with the pommel. When the pommel is used as a weapon to strike the adversary, it becomes a part of the "hammer" mentioned earlier. In addition to this, the pommel is like the rudder of your sword. You use it to control the motion of your point. This will be discussed more in Section II.

Quillons

The *quillons*, pronounced kee-yawN, is also referred to as the cross guard. The word's origin is obscure, but it most likely comes from an old French or Latin word for reed. The purpose of the quillons is to protect your hands from a downward cut and separate the blade from the handle. They are indispensable when defending or attacking. For example, you can use the quillons to spike an opponent's vital areas at close range or deflect and control an opponent's blade from a farther distance. The quillons always run perpendicular to the blade. While sometimes straight, they can also be curved: either downward to the point, inward to the pommel or in an S shape.

The Handle

The handle is the section between the pommel and the quillons. This is the part of the sword that you hold onto when you are swinging it. The handle can be made of wood and may be wrapped in leather. It may also be sandwiched between antler, slats of wood or some other material for grip but that depends on personal preference.

The Hilt

The hilt includes the pommel, the quillons and the handle. Today, people sometimes use the phrase "to the hilt" to refer to doing something all the way. Traditionally, the phrase describes what happens when a swordsman sticks his sword so far into his target that the hilt comes in contact with it. It's a gory little metaphor but apt. The offensive and defensive use of the hilt will be discussed more in this section and Section II.

The Blade

In movies and novels, the blade of the sword is the part that is most commonly used to strike with. The long sword has a straight blade, which is divided into three sections: the forte, the *mezza* (the middle) and the foible. The long sword is a two-sided weapon, and both sides are sharp. The saying "it's a double-edged sword" refers to double-edged Western European blades, meaning that you can cut both ways without the need to turn it like you do with a single-edged sword.

The edge facing away from your body and toward your adversary is known as the "true edge." It's also sometimes referred to as the "long edge." If you rotate the sword in your hands or flip sides, the true edge is still the part of the blade that is downward.

The "false edge," sometimes known as the "back edge" or "short edge," is the part of the blade that faces your body and does not face your adversary. The false edge is always the edge closest to the webbing of the thumbs. There are many offensive and defensive techniques for the back edge, but we will not discuss them in this beginner's guide.

It's important to know where the edges of your blade are during a fight so that you always strike an adversary with a sharp edge rather than the flat of the blade.

Long Sword Blade vs. Katana Blade

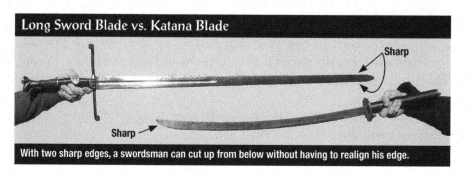

With two sharp edges, a swordsman can cut up from below without having to realign his edge.

15

The Forte

When a composer wants a musician to play a note loudly, he adds a forte sign to his composition. When the military wants to be in a strong, defensive position, they usually build a fort. Pronounced for-TAY or fort, the forte comprises the first third of the blade, starting from the quillons.

The forte is the slowest part because it's the closest part to the swordsman's hands. To illustrate this concept, the Renaissance Italian instructor Giacomo di Grassi wrote in his book *His True Art of Defence* (1594) that students should think of the sword as moving in a circle; their hands are the middle of the circle while the points of their swords represent the circle's circumference. The forte, which is closest to the hands, moves a lot slower than the point on the circumference.

The forte is the best defense for a swordsman because it is the slowest and strongest part of the blade. The forte doesn't need to move very fast. Because it's so close to the body, this makes it a swordsman's most effective defense. The forte's edges are generally dull because it's meant to take blows with as little damage to the edges as possible. If the forte was sharp, a swordsman might run the risk of nicking or notching the blade and thus weakening the weapon. Also, if a swordsman were to strike with the forte, it would be more like striking with a club than cutting with a sword.

As stated above, the forte is the slowest part of the blade, and this is a simple matter of a fulcrum and a lever. The forte is closest to your hands so it is at the beginning of the lever. When swinging the sword, a small movement of the forte can translate into a large movement of the point. This means that you can utilize an economy of motion in our strikes, and still move the sword to where it will defend or offend in the best possible manner. This will be discussed more in Section II.

The Mezza

The mezza is an Italian word that means "middle." Here, it refers to the middle third of the sword that your point and pommel rotate around. Think of it as the part that swordsmen swing at each other when their swords cross.

Once the swords cross, the two swordsmen have a moment to decide what they will do next.

The Foible

Foible (FOY-ble) is another word that has carried over to modern language from the past. If you hear someone talking about another person's foibles, he would be talking about that person's weaknesses. Therefore, the foible on a sword is its weakest defensive part. Opponents attack the sword's foibles to get the upper hand.

The foible is the last third of the blade and is the farthest part from the hilt. Because it is located so far from a swordsman's hands, the foible can offer no defense against an opponent who uses the forte to attack.

However, the foible is the fastest part of the blade because it is at the end of the "lever." A small movement of the hands will translate into a large and quick movement with the foible. This makes the foible perfect for fast attacks like cuts or thrusts.

The Sweet Spot

The sword is like a large knife. If you take a good steak knife and push the edge straight down onto a steak, you will crush the meat but you may not cut it. If you pull or push the knife at the same time that you are pushing down, you cut the meat. The sword works the same way. The sword is a precision cutting tool, not a crushing tool. When an attack is made, you

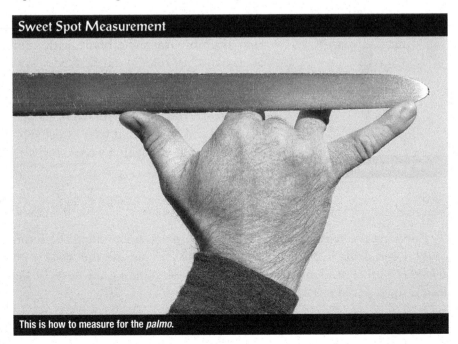

Sweet Spot Measurement

This is how to measure for the *palmo*.

Sweet Spot Measurement

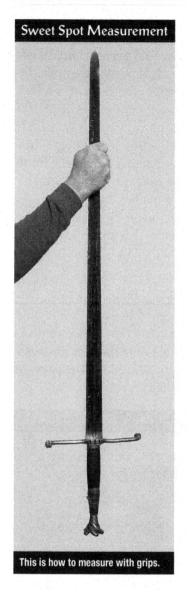

This is how to measure with grips.

strike the adversary with the blade in a precise way in order to pull or push the blade with the hilt to cut.

I like to call this part the "sweet spot" because it is the best place to cut your adversary with. You may hear it also called the "center of percussion" by other instructors.

The sweet spot is different for each person, and there are two ways to find it. The first way is by using an old Italian unit of measure called a *palmo*. The palmo is proportional to each individual. If you "hang 10," stretching your thumb and pinkie as far as you can, this is a palmo. Place your pinkie on the point of your sword and stretch the thumb as far down the blade as you can without removing the pinkie from the point. Grasp your blade just under your thumb, and you have found the sweet spot.

The other way to find your sweet spot is to grasp your blade in the palm of your hand with the point resting in the bend of your thumb. Grasp the blade with your other hand just under your first grip. Now release your top hand and place it again on the blade under your second grip. Once you release the blade with your second grip, you will have found your sweet spot. You can measure it again by checking with your palmo.

Knowing the parts of the sword will help you understand the information and drills in Sections II and III. As you discuss this book with friends or other students, you'll see how understanding the parts of the sword makes study easier.

Chapter 2:
Know the Line

Imagine that you are standing in front of a mirror, facing an "adversary." Hold out your arms, but keep your elbows tucked to your side and make sure that your pinkie fingers are facing out. You are now looking at all the area that you will need to defend.

Now drop your left hand. Pretend your right hand is your sword. Notice how your "sword" arm is pointing to your reflection's left side and blocking your adversary's view of your right side. You've just closed off your adversary's line of attack and defended your outside body line.

There are two types of lines that we will talk about in this chapter: lines of the body and lines of attack. Each swordsman has lines of the body and lines of attack. However, we will only discuss how these lines affect you because protecting yourself is your foremost concern while fighting; you are the most important person in the world. If you continue your studies, you will learn how to manipulate your lines and those of your opponent to your advantage. You will also learn more about this in Section III.

Lines of the Body

Lines of the body are lines that you want to defend. They also tell you when a line is open and where the attack will come from. They consist of the outside, inside, high and low line.

In this chapter, I'll explain these lines in greater detail and how you can open and close a defensive line. An open line is a line that the sword is not in. A closed line is a line that your sword is in.

To understand the lines of the body, let's go back to the mirror you were standing in front of with your right arm extended in front of you. Your hand is pointing to your reflection's left side and blocking your right side from view.

The imaginary line that starts at your weapon hand and runs along the outside of that arm to your shoulder is the "outside line." In the mirror, your outside line is currently "closed" because your sword would block any attempted attacks.

The imaginary line that you would draw from your weapon hand to your opposite shoulder along the inside of the weapon arm is the "inside line." In the mirror, your inside line is currently "open" to attack because

Lines of the Body

The gray area represents the high line, and the black area represents the low line. The dotted pattern represents the inside line, and the "X" pattern represents the outside line.

your sword is "in" or protecting the outside line. To close your inside line, hold your extended arm across your body. Now the inside line is closed, but the outside line is open.

Anytime you close a line of the body, you open another. There is no way to help this. However, you can use this knowledge to manipulate your adversary. If you intentionally open a line, then you dictate where the adversary will attack, which gives you control of the fight.

In addition to the outside and inside lines, there are the high and low lines, which are split at the waist.

From the waist up is the "high line." If you hold your sword with the point up, you close your high line. If you hold your sword too high, then you can open your high line and low line. In some techniques, the swordsman intentionally opens the high and low line because the speed and power of the descending blow makes the risk acceptable.

From the waist down is the "low line." If you hold your sword with the point down, then you close your low line. We will not spend much time learning to defend the low line because the low line is usually protected through the use of footwork. We will discuss this aspect more in this section.

Just because you open or close your inside or outside line doesn't mean that your high or low lines are automatically protected. Let's go back to the mirror scenario in which you are standing with your sword hand extended in front of you. In this situation, your high outside line is closed, but your high inside line is open. If you were to lower your arm so it points to the floor, then your low outside line is closed, but your low inside line is open and your high inside and outside line would also be unprotected.

Lines of Attack

You need to know open and closed lines in order to understand how lines of attack work.

Lines of attack are the lines you use to launch an attack at your adversary. If you drew a line from your pelvis to your adversary, then that is your line of attack. You want it to be straight so it's the most direct and shortest path to your adversary. You want your adversary's line of attack to not be straight and directly targeted to you.

Let's say that you are standing directly across from an adversary. You both have long swords in your right hands, closing the high outside line from each other. At the moment, you each have the same line of attack. If you were to swing your swords, starting over your heads, and bringing them down, then you'd both be hit and the story would end right there.

Your goal is to move so that your line of attack, which extends out from your center, is aimed directly at your adversary. You want his line of attack, which also extends from his center, to be aimed at something else.

You change your line of attack with footwork, which we will discuss in the next chapter and Chapter 8.

Beware, closing a line too far (moving your sword too far to the outside or inside on your defense or too high or too low) makes you vulnerable. It will take your sword longer to recover the open line, leaving yourself vulnerable to a deadly attack.

If you are aware of this, you can pretend to give your adversary an open line to attack.

When you close a line of attack, you only have to close it just enough to protect you from the strike. If the strike misses you by an inch, then it may as well have missed you by a mile.

Chapter 3:
Standing Tall With Proper Stance

While studying in Europe, my class would practice proper stance at the beginning of every class. My teacher would say, "Everyone, sit on the edge of your barstool, with a keg between your knees and a pint in your extended hand." We didn't have barstools or kegs in class, but my instructor used that phrase because people could easily understand the body mechanics of that position. When you sit on the edge of a chair or stoop, your hips roll forward, which straightens out the spine and keeps the shoulders over the hips. The "keg" forced us to keep our knees bent because holding something large and round between your knees makes it very difficult to straighten them. Holding our "pint" would give us something to imagine holding in our hands while we kept our arms extended.

The stance you take should balance you, allowing you to move quickly when needed or give you a sturdy platform from which to launch an attack. Your foot placement, bent knees and stance determine where you move, how you move, how fast you move and which direction you can attack from. If your feet are too close together, your balance is very narrow. If your feet are too far apart, you may not be able to recover your balanced base after you have moved.

You Really Have Four Legs

Foot placement gives a swordsman good balance.

To learn how to place your feet, put a square that is the width of your shoulders on the floor. Everyone is built differently, so the square that you practice on may not be exactly the same size as someone else's. Once the square is in place, position one foot on a front corner of the box and the other foot on the opposite back corner.

When your feet are properly place on the corners of the square and your sword is in front of you and between you and your adversary, you should have four legs, figuratively speaking. The first two are your legs, which are on diagonal corners of the square, and the other two are invisible legs, which are on the other two corners. By positioning your legs correctly, you will be well balanced and can move in any direction easily. This strength of position gives you a stronger and more secure stance from any angle.

You do not have strength of position if you can't move easily in any

Proper Foot Placement

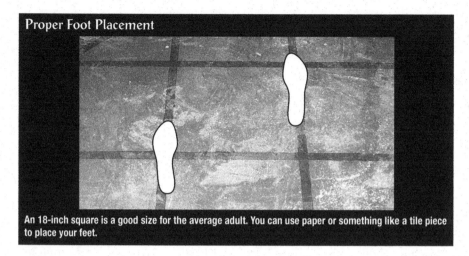

An 18-inch square is a good size for the average adult. You can use paper or something like a tile piece to place your feet.

direction and are unbalanced. Reconsider the square. If you place your back foot directly behind the front foot, meaning both feet are placed on complementary corners and not diagonal opposites, then you can only easily move forward and back; this is known as the "fencing stance." If you place your feet on the two front corners of the square so they are parallel, you can move strongly from side to side but not forward and back; this is known as "horse stance."

Having "four" legs allows you to keep the strengths of both the fencing and horse stances. It will also keep your hips angled and aimed straight toward your adversary. Having your hips facing your adversary not only helps in your movement but also gives you the greatest amount

Improper Foot Placement

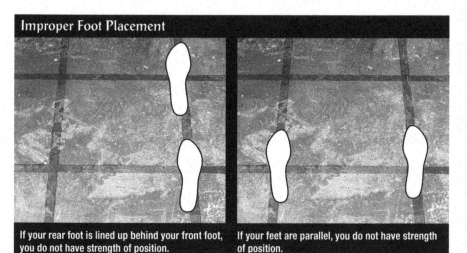

If your rear foot is lined up behind your front foot, you do not have strength of position.

If your feet are parallel, you do not have strength of position.

Proper Hip Placement

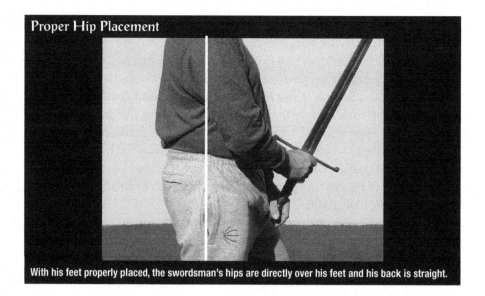

With his feet properly placed, the swordsman's hips are directly over his feet and his back is straight.

of strength in your strikes; this is your best line of attack. Because your hips are angled toward your adversary, you can use your sword to close the line that is being attacked, and you can also move and change your angle more easily.

Changing angles can also close a line that is being attacked by moving off of it. When you change an angle, you change the line of attack that your adversary is striking you on. By changing this line of attack, you move to a position that puts your sword between his attack and your body. This can also put you in a position that makes your attack more likely to succeed.

The same is true for attacking the adversary. If you have four legs, it is easier for you to move to a different line of attack because you have more freedom of movement. This ability to move will allow you to change your line of attack and strike at your adversary from an angle that will make it difficult for him to defend himself.

Each Foot's Job

In the proper stance, each foot has a job to help control the body.

The lead foot, or the foot that is positioned slightly in front of the other, controls the shoulder. The shoulders will naturally want to go where the lead foot is pointing. It is possible to point your foot in one direction and move in another, but you end up fighting your own body, which takes time and concentration away from the rest of the fight. If the lead foot is turned toward the left, your shoulders will turn in that direction, too. The same is true if the toes are turned toward the right, the shoulders will follow their direction. Note: Whether the lead foot is the left or right foot depends entirely on personal preference and circumstance.

The rear foot, which is the foot positioned behind the lead, controls the hips. If you turn your rear heel while pivoting on the ball of the foot, you will move your hips slightly. Pivoting on the heel of your foot while moving your toes in a circular motion, you will move your hips and widen you stance. Whether you choose to pivot on your heel or your toe is a tactical consideration that needs to be made at the time and can change from situation to situation.

When you are in your proper stance, always point the big toe of your lead foot toward your adversary. By doing this, you will keep your hips and shoulders angled toward your adversary, and the direction of your toe will tell the rest of your body which direction you are moving toward. If your toe is pointed to the side of your adversary, then that is where your blows and movement will be directed. Your lead foot controls the angle of your shoulders and the angle of the shoulders in turn guides your hands, which control your sword.

Just as you need to tell your shoulders where to go with your lead foot, you tell your body where to go with your rear foot. Because your rear foot controls your hips, your body will naturally want to step in the direction that your hips are pointing. You can point your hips in one direction and move in another, but this takes precious time and momentarily sacrifices your balance. If your adversary sees you lose balance, he may be able to take advantage of it and attack you. If you are struggling to maintain your balance, it is more difficult to close the line that is being attacked.

Bend At The Knees, Not The Waist

Your knees are your shock absorbers. If you are in the correct stance, they allow you to move quickly and smoothly in any direction. By bending more or straightening your knee, you are able to adjust your distance by small amounts without actually moving your feet. These small adjustments in the flex and bend of your knees move your body slightly, changing your distance in relation to your adversary.

If your legs are straight, you must bend them to be able to move. Stand with your weight on the balls of your feet and mostly toward your lead foot, but with your heels resting lightly on the ground. To see if your legs are positioned properly, stand with your feet on the two corners of your square. With your knees slightly bent, try lifting your heels off the ground, one at a time like you're walking, without moving your shoulders up and down; your shoulders should be level and steady. This is only a test to check your balance.

Keeping your knees straight and bending them when you are preparing to move gives your intentions away and lets your adversary know that you are planning on moving. If you give your intentions away, your adversary can hit you while you are moving.

Be careful that you do not bend so much that your knees go past your toes because this pressure can cause long-term damage to your knees.

In addition, don't lean forward at the waist. Doing so will off-balance your center because your weight will not be placed over your hips. Also, bending at the waist can bring your head into your adversary's striking range. If you bend at the knees, you can still gain the distance that you need, but you keep your balance over your feet.

Also, if you are leaning at the waist you must pull your head back over your feet before you are able to move. This will take time, and it will also give your adversary the opportunity to see your movement and counter before you have completed it.

Moving In Your Stance

You need to move with your four legs in order to maintain your center of gravity over your feet. Think of it this way: If you tense your gluts while walking, your hips automatically roll forward. Your body follows your center of gravity rather than your feet. When in your stance, you can move forward by rolling your hips forward and shifting your weight to the front foot. Once your lead knee reaches your lead toe, the momentum will move your body while keeping you balanced in your stance. Moving in this fashion allows you to maintain your balance and stance, so your center moves parallel with the ground without bouncing you up and down as you move.

If you roll your hips back, your weight shifts behind you and on your heels. If your center of gravity is behind your heels, you can move backwards quickly and easily, but you cannot move forward. Note: if your balance is always behind you, and your adversary sees this, he'll take advantage of the situation to push you off-balance.

After moving, make sure you end in a good strong stance before moving again. Doing so provides you with mobility, strength and protection.

The Gorilla Walk

When a student is learning proper footwork, I use the gorilla walk as drill and visual tool to teach him how to move his body in unison. This gives him the greatest strength possible in his actions.

When a gorilla walks, he moves his shoulders and his hips together so that the shoulder is always over the hip. The gorilla doesn't cross his body so that his right hip and left shoulder are forward. When the gorilla's right leg is forward so is his right shoulder.

If you move your hips without your shoulders, only your hips will face your adversary when you move. The reason I don't want you to do this is because, if you do, you will not be able to use your body to help strengthen your strikes and defenses. When you make an attack, the attack is not only powered with your arms but also with the weight of your body. If you move your shoulder and hip together when you make a strike, you will put your weight behind the strike and not have to rely only on the strength of your arms.

Besides adding strength to your strike, moving your body as a whole also helps you maintain your balance and ability to continue your movement.

When you want to make a strike with your sword, your lead shoulder and hip (this is your sword arm, which is either the right or left one depending on your dominate arm) should move forward toward your target. If you want to grapple with your adversary, your left hip and shoulder should move forward to give you the necessary distance. If you move your right hip and your left shoulder forward at the same time, you reduce the distance that you can reach with your rear hand.

Think of the saying: "Your foot supports your hand, and your hand protects your foot." If you don't move your limbs together, you run the risk of your adversary twisting your body. If your leg is not supporting your shoulder, let's say you're right shoulder is not over your left hip, your adversary can push you around and your balance will be compromised. If your adversary puts himself in a weak stance, you can twist him into a weaker position.

Chapter 4:
Movement and Math

In Filippo Vadi's treatise *Arte Gladiatoria*, he illustrates in a drawing a man standing on a wagon wheel to represent the movement of the feet, a sun next to the right foot to represent the rotation of that foot, and a tower next to the left foot to represent the other foot's stability. In the 16th and 17th centuries, however, masters like Achille Morrozo and Gerard Thibault wrote treatises using geometry and math to explain the movements and angles necessary for a sword fight. Even William Shakespeare refers to the use of mathematics in sword fighting.

Geometry—the interplay of objects in a three-dimensional space—is a big part of martial practice. When you are in a sword fight, both the combatants and swords move. Understanding the geometry of the fight helps you understand the best place for you to be and the best time for you to attack.

The three shapes of geometry relevant to sword fighting are the square, the circle and the triangle.

The Square

We use the square to help us with our footwork. The square that was placed on the ground in the previous chapter showed you how to place your feet while stationary. If you take that square and multiply it so that the entire floor is covered in a grid pattern, you can then move from one square to another while fighting. By moving like this, you maintain your stability and strength of position, which allows you to easily move in any direction.

As you saw in the previous chapter, you'll have four legs as you move from square to square if you use proper balance and footwork. Different systems and arts stand on different sides of the square, but all sword-fighting systems use this principle. For example, modern sport fencing keeps the feet on the same side of the square. As we study the use of the long sword, we will have one foot on the front corner of the square and the other foot on the opposite back corner of the square. By understanding what part of the square the adversary is standing on, you will have a better understanding of where his balance is weak. This understanding allows you to move away from where he's well protected and target his weaknesses, making your path to victory easier. (Note: In Section II, I'll discuss moving squares as transitioning guards.)

The Circle

Every blow of your sword, whether it is a cut or a thrust, is part of a circle. If you look at a downward movement of the blade, which travels from shoulder to hip, you'll note how it moves in a circular fashion. If you continue the movement, you'll bring the sword back to the starting point by closing the circle.

But what about a thrust? The thrust is a straight line, right? Not really. It's actually part of a very small circle on the vertical or horizontal plane. When you thrust your sword out, the blade descends or ascends on the vertical plane, or moves from left to right or right to left on the horizontal, creating a half-circle. When you pull it back, this completes the circle.

The Triangle

When you strike at your adversary, one of three things happens: You hit him, his sword deflects your attack, or you miss him. If you hit him or his sword, the place that your sword crosses his body or sword creates a triangle.

Once you see where a triangle is created, you can move so that you have leverage over his blade, or you can choose to yield to his strength while moving to a different square so that you have a better line of attack on him. If you close distance with your adversary, you can use the triangle to manipulate his body at the joints. At close range, you can perform arm locks, manipulate his balance and use other techniques to weaken your adversary's position.

All these shapes come together to help you move correctly. If you are aware of how to use and manipulate the geometry of fighting, you can make your adversary weaker than you. If he is in a weaker position than you, you don't need to try to be physically stronger to beat him.

Chapter 5:
Measure

Measure (distance) is one of the most important factors in any fight. If you are too close to your adversary, you can get hit without being able to protect yourself because his attack will take less time than your counter. If you are too far away from your adversary, he won't be able to hit you, but you won't be able to hit him either. If you attempt to attack the adversary while he is out of range, you can throw yourself out of place and balance.

Distance is gained and lost by advancing, retreating and traversing. When you traverse, you step off the line of attack and to the side of your adversary, creating a new line of attack. You can move from side to side, forward and backward. If you move from side to side, you can change the distance and line of attack, along with opening lines on your adversary.

The optimal distance from your adversary is determined by many factors. The length of your weapon is one factor that will determine your distance. When faced with an attacker whose sword is longer, it's a common mistake to try to stay farther away from him. This is because this places you out of your ideal distance and into his ideal distance in that you have no option to attack but he does. Because he has the longer weapon, he can force you back and cut off your mobility. He'll always be in range to strike you, but you'll never be in range to hit him.

Types of Distance

Joseph Swetnam was a fencing master who taught Henry, the Duke of Wales, who was also brother to Charles I. In his treatise *The School of the Noble and Worthy Science of Defence* published in 1617, he discusses distance:

> To know the place, this may be taken three ways, as this, the place of thy weapons, the place of defence and the place of offense: ... but it is chiefly meant here as the place of offense; thou must mark which is the nearest part of thine enemy towards thee, and which lyeth most unregarded, whether it be his dagger hand, his knee or his leg, or where thou maist best hurt him at a large distance without danger to thyself.

This quote mentions two types of measure. The first measure is between you and your adversary (how far you need to move to hit your adversary). The second measure is to your closest target that the adversary leaves undefended for you, like an open line no matter whether the target is his arm, head or any other part. Your measure is also affected by the angle you have in relation to your adversary.

When considering target measure (the second distance), be aware of which target you choose. If your adversary swings down at your head, it would be foolish to attack his leg. If you were to attack his leg, you would put yourself in his line of attack, and your sword would not be between his sword and your body. As a result, you would most likely be hit in the head. In this scenario, your better target options are to attack a part of his body that will put your sword between his sword and your body for defense. You could also attack him before his cut is fully developed, disrupting his tempo, which will be discussed in the following chapter.

Your Angle and Your Measure

We talked about angles used for balance in Chapter 3. In this section, we discuss how angles are used for measure.

The line of attack you take also determines the distance you are from your adversary. One way that you can change your line is to traverse. When you traverse, you change the angle of the line of attack between you and your adversary and also change the target measure. For example, your adversary has his sword closing his high line and the outside line on his right side. You are directly in his line of attack and on the defensive. To turn tables, you traverse to the left, moving to your left and beyond his outside line. By just changing the angle of your attack with footwork, you're in a better position to continue the fight.

The way you step, regardless of the foot you're moving, changes both your striking range and the line between you and your adversary. Your reach is affected by which foot you have forward because it determines which shoulder is forward. If you have your rear foot forward, your sword will need to come across your body and your reach will be shorter. If you have your sword foot forward, your reach will be longer.

Practice using and changing angles and measure in all your practice. If you aren't aware of how your movement affects your angle and measure, you may put yourself in a very dangerous position. If you are attacking, the angle and measure that you step to will either lengthen or shorten the time that it takes to make your attack.

Reach and Measure

right

left

With the right foot and shoulder forward, your reach is extended and measure shortened.

With the left foot and shoulder forward, your reach is shortened and your measure is lengthened.

You Control The Measure

During matches and fights, it is important for you to fight to your distance and not to allow your adversary to control the distance, meaning you always want your adversary to react to your measure. You can control your distance by stepping in with both feet, stepping back or stepping to either side. Never close the distance with your adversary when you are on the defensive, and never attack when you are out of range because you will miss your adversary.

Using distance to your advantage is easy to learn but hard to perfect. Once you understand how to use measure, it becomes second nature and is much more effective than bending at the waist and reaching to strike your adversary. I will give you an example of how you can use distance for defense and attack.

If your adversary cuts at your head, you can use distance as a defense by stepping out of range with your lead foot. Do not step too far back with your foot, only far enough so that you are beyond the reach of his weapon. Generally you only need to bring your lead foot as far back as your rear foot and out to the side, leaving your feet on the back two corners of your "box". This will help you maintain a strong stance and allow you to move your foot again for a counterattack.

As his blade goes by you, you can use the back edge of your blade to strike it in the same direction it was already traveling. When you do this, you are using the strength he has exerted, and adding a little bit of your own, to push his weapon farther past you than he was planning. As his sword moves away, you can step in and attack your adversary.

In this example, all you had to do was move one foot back and tap your adversary's sword with your edge as it went by and then bring your foot forward again to hit your adversary's by returning your sword on the same line that it traveled the first time.

Chapter 6:
Tempo

Every attack and defensive action requires a certain amount of time to complete, regardless of whether it's a sword technique or a step. Measure is the distance that you are from your adversary, but it also helps to control the tempo of a fight.

Tempo refers to timing. When you are facing your adversary, the time that you keep is how long a particular move, step or action takes.

While a step might seem like a very quick thing, a step can be a slow process that can cost you in a fight. Your tempo in a fight is what allows you to move around your adversary and his weapon.

Let's consider two antagonists, Tom and Jerry, who are evenly matched in all respects—their weapons, training and speed are the same. When Tom attacks, it is up to Jerry to see the attack and react. When Jerry sees the attack, his eyes have to send the message to his brain that an attack is coming. His brain tells his arms to protect him, and his arms move to do so.

When you use tempo, you watch your adversary's movements and counter them at the same time he attacks. Or, if you defend a move on his time and counterattack on a different time, the adversary has to try to catch up to defend your attack.

Tempo happens really fast. Ed McGiveren, a 1930s rancher in Montana who studied the quick draw, theorized in his book *Fast and Fancy Revolver Shooting* that the quickest possible draw was 0.3 seconds. This means that in three seconds, a gunfighter realizes he's behind his opponent in drawing, sends that signal to his brain who returns it to his hand to draw. Even in those 0.3 seconds, the defending gunfighter will always be slower than the gunfighter who initiated the draw.

Three Types of Time

In this book, we discuss the three types of time found in the Italian style:

- *dui tempe* (two time)
- *stesso* tempo (single time)
- *mezzo* tempo (half time)

Dui tempe or "two time" is a concept that we see in modern fencing today. The best way to describe this tempo is to think of "parry and riposte"

Dui Tempe

counterattack

defend

In dui tempe, you defend the attack then counterattack.

or "defend and then counterattack." Dui tempe is the easiest and safest time to use, but it is also the slowest tempo.

In stesso tempo or "single time," you launch a counterattack to protect yourself from an attack. If your adversary attacks you, instead of defending yourself, you counter into his line of attack. By attacking into his line, you simultaneously go on the offensive and defend yourself by

Stesso Tempo

defend and counter

In stesso tempo, you defend at the same time that you attack.

stopping his strike. Stesso tempo is the second hardest time to use, but it is faster then dui tempe.

Mezzo tempo or "half time" is the hardest time to use in a fight, but it is also the fastest. Before your adversary can fully develop an attack, you attack him. Let us suppose that you are facing your adversary. He begins to shift his weight forward to initiate an attack. As soon as his weight begins to shift, you attack him. I like to think of it like this: If he twitches, hit him. That strategy won't hold up in a court of law, but it works in a sword fight. Another example: When your adversary is shifting from one position to another, you strike him. George Silver, in his treatise *Paradoxes of Defence* (1599), calls this "the time of hand over foot."

Mezzo Tempo

attack

attack

In mezzo tempo, you attack before your adversary completes his attack.

When you are countering your adversary's attack, you can create one of these three tempos by moving your sword or feet. You can use measure and angles to help you take advantage of, or create, tempo.

You can also use an adversary's tempo against him by attacking him while he's moving. The second way is to change the timing of the fight away from his time to your time.

If you would like to change the timing of a fight, work at his time and then suddenly change the time or tempo of the fight. To illustrate this, you need at least two people to clap together. As you are clapping to a beat (1&2&3&4&...), your partner will double clap so that he changes the tempo of the clap. He gets two claps in while the you only clap once. The same will work with an attack. If you are both fighting at the same tempo, then you get a quick second attack in while your adversary gets only one attack or defense in. You have changed the tempo of the fight. I like to ask my students whose time they should fight too. The correct answer to that question is "mine." Never fight to your adversary's time; always fight to your time.

Do Not Swing Your Sword Too Wide

When you are attacking and moving, you are looking at how an adversary defends, moves and counterattacks. It is important that you do not overswing while you are doing this. If your attack is too wide, your adversary can step to one side or the other and change the line of attack. This can lengthen the tempo of your attack. Or if he steps into the attack, he can shorten your tempo and attack into your sword. He can then take leverage over your sword by striking your flat with the edge of his sword.

If you overswing or cut past him because you put too much power into your attack, your adversary can change distance to his advantage before you can bring your weapon between the two of you. For example, you attack with too much power and your adversary steps away from the attack, which changes the distance so that your attack misses him. After your sword goes past him, he steps back into the proper measure to hit you. You may not have time to get your sword back in place before he hits you. You would be unable to defend yourself because the amount of tempo you would need to get your sword back into place for your defense would take longer than the amount of time it would take your adversary to hit you. This is the primary use of tempo. You don't need to move fast; you just need to move at the right tempo.

Steaphen Fick

Chapter 7:
Wadda Ya Look at in a Fight?

Some people say to look at the adversary's eyes, but this is a mistake. If you are looking at your adversary's eyes, there is a tendency to believe he will strike where he's looking. It is possible to lie with your eyes and make people believe that you are going to strike somewhere that you are not intending to attack. Also, if you are looking at your adversary's eyes, you can be drawn into his gaze and lose your peripheral vision because you are focusing on one point. Another problem with watching the eyes is that sword fighters often wear masks or helmets for protection. If you are trained and accustomed to looking at the eyes for clues about the strikes but can't see them, you can lose orientation and slow your movements. It only takes a fraction of a second to get hit.

Another place that people believe they should look is at the sword. If you are looking at the sword and tracking the motion of the blade with your eyes, you may not be aware of the rest of your adversary's body or your surroundings. When you look at the sword, you are more aware of the point than of the hilt. If you are watching the point of the blade, it will move too fast for you to follow and protect yourself from. You will also find that if you are trying to watch the point of your adversary's sword, you will lose sight of it in different light conditions and backgrounds. In addition, if you are concentrating on following the point of the sword with your eyes, you won't have time to think of other things, like your defense or movement.

The Chest

If you are looking at the chest of your adversary, you can see his shoulders, hips, arms, feet and hilt. Being able to see his shoulders can tell you what type of movement he is about to make. Being able to see his feet can alert you to how he is probably going to move, and if you can see his hilt, you have an idea of where the point will be coming from because the point is connected to the pommel.

Learning to look in one spot but not focus on it takes practice. Once you have become accustomed to "seeing" your entire adversary, you can vary the places that you look at, but your eyes should always stay in the area of the chest.

39

To Look vs. To See

To "look" is to see and to "see" is to understand. If you look at what an adversary is doing but do not understand it, you run a greater risk of getting hit. If you understand what you are seeing, then you will know how to counter what they are doing.

Look at the middle of your adversary's chest but don't focus on that point. While you are looking at his chest, you want to "see" the rest of his body and the surrounding area.

If you pick an object to look at, you can see observe the object. Let's say that you are looking at a picture on the wall. If you only focus on that picture, will you be able to see what is happening around the picture? Will you see the cat passing by? How about the person who is entering your room? In a fight, it is important to be aware of people and objects around you so you won't be surprised by something. This is how to use your peripheral vision while fighting. You can find a drill to help you practice using your peripheral vision in the last chapter in Section II.

Chapter 8:
On Defense

In movies, we see sword fighters plant their feet firmly on the ground before swinging their sword around in a "Cuisinart of death." This works great as long as the bad guys don't fight back. If the bad guys are nice enough to run into the hero's sword instead of attacking the hero's body, our hero will emerge triumphant.

A complete defense is divided into two halves: footwork and sword movement. It is possible to defend yourself with only one half, but the safest defense is a complete one in which both work together.

The Feet and the Sword

If the adversary is trying to hit you, you cannot afford to plant your feet in one place and stand your ground. Instead, you use footwork to constantly change your position throughout a fight. This is the safest and surest way to move out of your adversary's line of attack and into your own. There are eight directions that you can move. You can move straight forward, straight back, forward right, forward left, right, left, back right or back left. Where you decide to move depends on the distance you want to be from your adversary and your current position. Footwork can also be used offensively by giving you a better angle to attack. The direction you step can also add power to your strikes.

However, be careful when you step toward your adversary. Even though stepping toward your adversary closes the measure and adds power to your strike, you may still be in your adversary's line of attack. Instead, use footwork to change your angle before attacking.

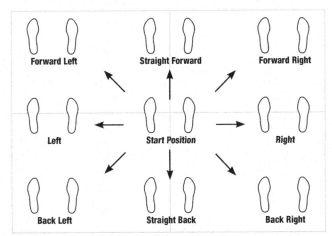

41

How you use your sword is as important an aspect in defense as how you move your feet. When you use your feet to change your angle and distance, you position your sword in a certain way. You will learn more about these specific positions in Chapter 9. Remember, how you move your sword affects your tempo. Larger movements lengthen the time it takes for you to launch counterattacks. By defending too wide, you might also become more focused on the sword rather than the man controlling the sword. Remember, your adversary controls his sword. Don't react to the sword; react to the man.

Block vs. Parry

There are two ways to intercept an attack: a block or a parry. Consider a punch.

If you block a punch, you raise your arm to stop it. There is a lot of force that hits your arm, and your defense depends on your ability to absorb your adversary's force with your own force.

If you parry a punch, you simply redirect your adversary's energy in the direction it was already going.

The concept of blocking and parrying is neither new nor unique to a specific martial art. If you parry an attack, you use your adversary's strength against him. If you block an attack, you pit your strength against your adversary's.

Webster's dictionary defines a block as an obstruction that makes passage or progress unsuitable. In swordplay, this is a defensive move that stops the attacker's action.

A very important rule to remember when you block is that you don't only stop your opponent's weapon but also your weapon. When you do this, you have lost the path and now have to start your movement again. (For more on the path, see Chapter 10.)

Let's suppose that your adversary attacks by bringing his sword down toward your head. Because you do not want to be hit by this attack, you need to either get out of the way or stop it. If you stop the movement of the attack, you have blocked it. By stepping into the attack and meeting his blade with your own, you reduce the power from the adversary's blow, but you also lose your power and momentum.

If you move in to defend an attack, you use all your muscles to stop both swords and then counterattack. This may not seem like it would require much effort, but when you are holding a three-pound sword out at arm's length while supporting the weight and force of another three-pound sword, your arms will get tired and sore. When you are tired, you slow down, and when you slow down, you get hit. It's not a good way to stay safe.

Proper Block

When blocking, you stop the movement of both swords.

When you parry an attack, you are not stopping the attack but "putting it aside."

Let's consider the same attack scenario that was used for a block.

When the adversary brings the sword down toward your head, you don't stop the attack. Instead, you raise your sword and deflect his attack to the side of your body. By parrying an attack, you redirect it away from you. The parry will allow you to take the power of his strike and move it

Proper Parry

When you parry an attack, you move the power of his strike outside your body so that you don't have to stop his power.

to the ground next to you or behind you. The parry is meant to allow you to continue the movement of your sword, transitioning your defensive action into an offensive one.

If you parry the adversary's attack, you can add power to his strike. Doing so is better for you because you can redirect his cut or thrust farther than he expected. This particular parry is known as the slap defense.

A parry takes less effort than a block, and a parry also helps you control the adversary's power and strength without giving up your power or strength.

Each of these techniques has advantages and disadvantages. It is important to understand how each of these aid you in a fight and how they may leave you exposed to another attack. I will not discuss every parry and block because that subject can take up a book all by itself—especially if we try to anticipate all possible attacks. This leads into the dangerous "what if" game, which does not help anyone because every move—regardless of how effective it is—has a counter.

Flat Or Edge?

Now that you know the differences between a block and parry, let's discuss a controversial topic—whether to defend with the flat of your sword or the edge.

The theory behind blocking with the flat is that doing so will not damage the edge of your blade. The proponents of the theory argue that because the sword is an expensive tool, you do not want to damage it by blocking with the edge. However, opponents of the theory argue that the flat is the weakest part of the sword to defend yourself with. A sword is maybe one-eighth of an inch thick, but it is 2 to 3 inches wide. If you block or parry with the flat, you are defending yourself with a very thin piece of metal.

Just Pulling Your Hilt

Remember back in Chapter 1 when you learned that cutting with a sword is similar to cutting with a steak knife? You don't press the knife down on the meat. Instead, you press down and pull the knife back toward you, slicing the meat open. In sword fighting, this is called pulling the hilt. To pull the hilt, strike at your adversary when transitioning guards and

Pulling the Hilt

The sword fighter pulls his hilt to block the adversary's attack.

then pull the blade back at the end of the transition. More to the point, you slice by pulling back on your pommel with your hands.

Pulling the hilt does several things. First, it allows you to cut rather than bash with your sword. Second, you are more effective with less effort. Third, you have the option of attacking or defending. If you defend, you pull your hilt to parry. If you attack, you pull your hilt to cut. (Remember, when you defend with your sword, you use the forte, and when you attack, you hit with the sweet spot.)

You can also push into the adversary's attack by thrusting your hilt out to redirect his force away from you or combine it with pulling your hilt. When you push an adversary's sword and then pull your hilt, your defensive action becomes offensive; you can now counterattack. For example, your adversary attacks your head with a downward strike. You push up your sword with the point still angled at your adversary, catching his blade on your hilt. Then pull your hilt back to slice at your adversary's head. Note that when you push your pommel up, you keep your sword at the same angle but move it into a higher line. This redirects the adversary's energy up and over your head, keeping you safe and making it more difficult for him to defend against your counterattack.

Section II

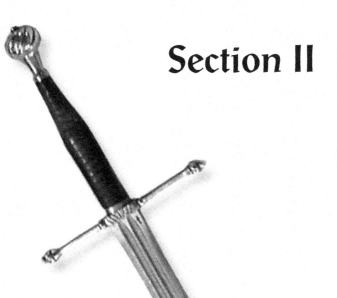

Practice With a Swordlike Object

Note to Reader:
The second section outlines the actions and movements of the long sword. It will help readers understand what they see in movies, television or in video games. The section includes drills that the reader can practice with sticks, practice swords or even plastic lightsabers. Of course, the reader should practice with caution no matter what.

Chapter 9:
Guards and Wards

Sword guards, or wards, are positions you transition into and out of during a fight. When you attack or defend, you change guards, and the same goes for your adversary. Both of you are always changing guards in reaction to the other. For example, let's say that you want to thrust to defend yourself against an adversary. In order to do so, you switch from the guard you're currently using to a new one. To respond to your transition, your adversary also changes guard.

Because guards are so important in offense and defense, don't focus on your adversary's sword in a fight. As he moves his sword, you may be tempted to chase his blade, which can leave your lines undefended or put you in awkward position. Instead, your sword should always end up between your body and your adversary's sword; your body and sword move together and not separately. To ensure that they do, move from one guard to another in the proper tempo.

In *Fiore di Battaglia*, Fiore dei Liberi describes a guard as a beginning and ending position of an aggressive action, meaning that it is the end of one action and the beginning of another. There are as many guards as there are known ways of striking. But in this book, we'll discuss the twelve main guards in *Fiore di Battaglia*. Each of the 12 guards can be placed into one of three categories: low guards, middle guards and high guards. We'll also discuss a 13th guard, which is not in the dei Liberi treatise and belongs in a category of its own.

This chapter is an ABC to guards. While it is easy to identify guards, it takes a long time to know how to effectively use them in combat.

Choosing Your Guard

When changing guards, your goal is to *invite an attack* from your adversary or make him *unable* or *unwilling* to attack. The guard your opponent chooses affects which guard you'll transition to. Likewise, the guard that you choose dictates his next action. By understanding the capabilities of your adversary's chosen guard, you will know which guard you can choose to control his reaction and targets.

For example, if you choose a guard that makes the adversary *unable to attack* you, your sword is in a guard that closes off his line of attack. He can't attack you from the guard that he is in because his sword will have to move through your sword, as it is positioned in your guard.

If you choose a guard that makes the adversary *unwilling to attack*, you have chosen a guard that does not close off the line of attack; his sword doesn't have to go through yours. However the guard you have chosen will place your sword between his attack and your body before his sword can reach you, like in dui tempe or stesso tempo. Even though he can attack you, it would be dangerous for him because your sword, in your chosen guard, will reach its target sooner.

If you want to *invite an attack*, choose a guard that makes your opponent believe that he has a clear line of attack to your body. The opening will be much larger than one that would make him unwilling to attack. When using a guard that leaves the opponent *unwilling to attack*, the adversary can see that a shift of your sword will give you the advantage. In the case of *inviting*, your goal is to make your adversary think he'll be able to complete his attack before you can stop him. In reality, all you have to do is shift the angle of your current guard and transition into another. You want to attack him while he's attacking, like in dui tempe. Because the guard he chooses will probably be an attack, the guard you transition into will depend on that.

The rest of this chapter breaks down certain guards used in a fight. For illustrative purposes, the guards transition in a specific order. During a fight, though, which guard you use will be determined by the events unfolding.

The Low Guards

These guards are called low guards because they close your low line and your sword is always pointed at the ground. The low guards are also the easiest to hold during a fight because you don't have to maintain a closed high line, so your arms don't get tired. In a fight, you use the low guards to begin a *sotani*, which is an ascending blow. To perform a sotani, move your point from a low line to a high line. The low guards are also used to complete a *fendente*, which is a descending blow. To perform a fendente, move your point from a high line to a low line.

The guard of the boar's tooth or the *denti di cinghiale* is a strong low guard used for developing thrusts and cuts. It earned its name because it moves much like a hunter would when attacking a boar. The attack is fast, and its low-guard position makes it easy for you to lift your sword and stick your adversary. Because of these factors, this guard generally makes an adversary unwilling to attack, but that doesn't mean that

Guard of the Boar's Tooth (Denti di Cinghiale)

denti di cinghiale
(DEN-tee dee CHINN-gal-lee)

the guard can't be used to make him unable to attack or invite him to attack. It all depends on variables like your ability, target and tempo. Note that in attacking, you transition out of the denti di cinghiale and into another guard.

In the denti di cinghiale, stand with your right foot forward so the lead toe faces the center of your adversary's body. (Note: If you are leading with your left hand, then the opposite applies.) Place your pommel on your left hip so the blade is angled downward and closes your low inside line. You want the point to be in your line of attack. Note that the false edge is facing your adversary. Because of how the sword is positioned, you need to widen your stance slightly for balance, which will also keep your hips and shoulders aimed at your adversary. For the low guards, this wider stance only applies to the denti di cinghiale and the *coda lunga*, which will be discussed soon.

From your position in the denti di cinghiale, you're going to transition into the *tutta porta di ferro* or the guard of the open iron door. Unlike the denti di cinghiale, the tutta porta di ferro invites the adversary to attack; the point of your blade is not between you and your adversary, making you appear vulnerable. The blade beckons the adversary like an open door that he can enter and exit at will. But, because this is a low guard-attack, your response to slam the door closed will be swift and unexpected.

To transition from denti di cinghiale to the tutta porta di ferro, step back with your right foot so that your left foot is now in front. Now, without moving the position of your lead hand, slide the pommel of your

Open Iron Door (Tutta Porta di Ferro)

tutta porta di ferro
(TOOT-ta por-TA dee FER-ro)

sword to the middle of your body, just under your navel. Note that your lead hand maintains its grip on the handle and your rear hand maintains its grip on the pommel. Your blade also changes position, moving in a semicircle to the right side. In the denti di cinghiale, the point is positioned between you and your adversary; it isn't here. Instead, the point of the blade is perpendicular or in line with your hips. This position of the blade leaves all of your lines open, which is the "open door." The "iron" part comes when you transition into another guard, probably middle or high, which brings your blade up swiftly in a sotani to close the door. Quite literally, your sword is the iron in this guard. (Also note: When in tutta porta di ferro, your true edge is angled toward your adversary.)

From the tutta porta di ferro, you're going to transition into the *mezza porta di ferro* or the guard of the middle iron door. This guard will seem like a mix of the tutta porta di ferro and the denti di cinghiale because

Middle Iron Door (Mezza Porta di Ferro)

mezza porta di ferro
(MEZ-za por-TA dee FER-ro)

of the position of your pommel and point. Like with the other iron door guard, the mezza porta di ferro slams the iron door with a sotani, closing off your adversary's line of attack. But because of its position, it can also be used to thrust. The mezza porta di ferro is also a guard that invites an adversary to attack or makes him unwilling to attack, depending on his level of awareness.

To transition from the tutta porta di ferro to the mezza porta di ferro, change the position of your feet. Technically, you could keep your left foot forward, but it's better to get used to moving in guards; always change your foot positioning with every transition. This is why you bring your right foot forward again for the mezza porta di ferro. Like the tutta porta di ferro, keep your pommel just under your navel. Also, move the point of your blade in front of you and place it directly between your legs. Because the point of the blade is more centered, you don't need to adopt a wider stance.

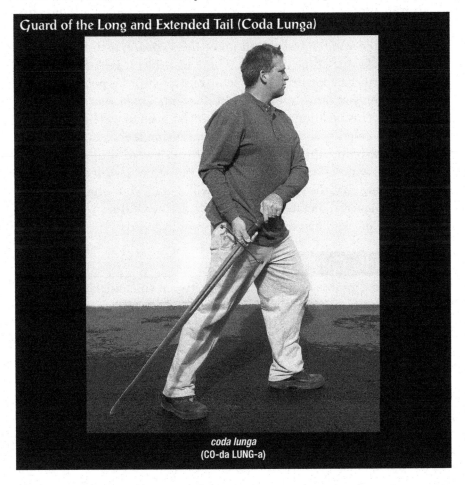

Guard of the Long and Extended Tail (Coda Lunga)

coda lunga
(CO-da LUNG-a)

53

From the mezza porta di ferro, you're going to transition into the coda lunga. The guard's full name is actually *posta di coda lunga e distesa*, which means "guard of the long and extended tail." For the purposes of the book, I'll refer to it simply as coda lunga.

Unlike the other low guards, the coda lunga hides how long your blade is. This makes it more difficult for the adversary to know his measure and gauge his striking distance. To achieve this, position your blade behind you like the tail of an animal. While the blade is behind you, the hilt is at your hip so you can strike quickly, if necessary. Like the tutta porta di ferro, the coda lunga opens all your lines to your adversary, inviting him to attack. However, you're still able to swiftly close his line of attack with a sotani. You can also thrust from the coda lunga because, even though the blade is positioned behind you, your sword is still in your direct line of attack.

To transition from the mezza porta di ferro to the coda lunga, first change the position of your feet so your left foot is now forward. Slide the pommel to your right hip and move the sword in a circular motion so the point is angled behind you. Think of it like this: Your body is a clock. At the mezza porta di ferro, the tip of your sword is positioned at 12 o'clock. When you move your sword to the coda lunga, you reposition it at 4 o'clock. This position also means that you need to widen your stance to maintain balance and keep your hips and shoulders squared to your adversary. Also note that the false edge of your sword is up.

You've now done the four low guards in the book with a right-hand lead. Be aware that the guards you use will dictate your angles and lines of attack. They also dictate how you move and what lines you can cover and close. Now, let's transition into the middle guards.

The Middle Guards

The middle guards keep your sword between you and your adversary and close your high line from your waist to your shoulders. For the most part, don't start a fight in a middle guard because the position of your sword will be obvious to your adversary. The point is more extended, and he can take advantage of it. Instead, you can use the middle guards to end an attack that began in a low guard or high guard. For example, you begin a sotani in a coda lunga and end in a middle guard, or you begin a thrust in a high guard then end in a middle guard. Ending an attack with a middle guard can also help you fight to your tempo because you can use them to intercept an adversary's attack. (For more on tempo, see

Chapter 6.) You can also pass through the middle guards to transition from a high guard to a low guard or vice versa.

The *posta breve* is the first of the middle guards you will look at. It is the easiest and most comfortable middle guard to use because it doesn't put stress on your arms. However, you need to use other middle guards as well. Otherwise, your adversary will catch on and be able to predict your movements. Like all middle guards, the posta breve is a good guard to end a sotani, fendente or thrust action from a high or low guard. You will perform your basic parry from the posta breve. (The basic parry will be discussed in greater detail in Chapter 14.) In regards to passing

Short Guard (Posta Breve)

posta breve
(PO-sta BRE-vay)

through a middle guard, the posta breve makes the adversary unwilling to attack because it's easy for you to defend all lines.

You'll transition from the coda lunga, which is a low guard, into the posta breve. For simplicity's sake, leave your feet where they are, even though you would normally want to change them. Next, slide your pommel to just below your navel. (Note that you're back in mezza porta di ferro.) To close your high line, bring your blade up and in front of your chest. The sword's true edge should be angled to face the line your adversary is threatening so he strikes the edge of your sword rather than the flat. The tip of the sword points upward at a steep angle. If your point is so low that it points at the adversary's chest or stomach, your adversary can take the opportunity to make you follow his tempo. At the same time, if you point too high, your arms are more vulnerable to an attack. No matter what, the elevation of your point and how far or close you hold your hilt to your body will vary from situation to situation. It takes time to learn what combinations will work best for you.

From the posta breve, you will transition into the *posta lunga* or the long guard. It is an uncomfortable guard to hold for a long time because your arms and your sword are fully extended. The posta lunga gives your adversary even more of a chance to control your sword and tempo than the posta breve.

Despite its drawbacks, the posta lunga protects you by giving you the necessary time to transition from a low guard to a high guard or vice versa. For example, let's say that you want to move from the low guard coda lunga into a high guard. To do so, you must transition from a low guard into a middle guard and then into the high guard. Because a step takes time, you use the extension of the posta lunga to keep the point of your sword in your adversary's face while you take the next step into the high guard. Obviously, this transition must be swift, but that's the purpose of practice.

To transition from the posta breve into the posta lunga, change the position of your feet so your right foot is now forward. Lower the tip of your sword so it points directly at your adversary's face. Next, extend your arms, so they are away from your body but still slightly lower than the point. Don't lock your joints or the weight of the sword could hyperextend your elbows. Instead, keep your elbows flexible so they act as shock absorbers when you strike. As a final note, angle the true edge of your sword directly into your adversary's line of attack.

From the posta lunga, you're going to transition into the *posta corona*.

Long Guard (Posta Lunga)

posta lunga
(PO-sta LUNG-a)

The guard's full name is actually *posta frontale o corona*, which translates as the "frontal guard of the crown (head)." For the purposes of this book, I'll refer to it simply as the posta corona.

Even though the posta corona looks like it should be a high guard, it's not. Unlike the high high guards, your sword is still directly between you and your adversary. The posta corona is a good example of how the guard you choose affects your adversary's reaction. If he's in a high guard, your posta corona makes him unable to attack because your high line is completely closed. If he's in a middle guard, your posta corona makes him unwilling to attack because you're probably taking control of the fight with tempo. If he's in a low guard, your posta corona invites him to attack because your low line seems vulnerable. While all these shades of gray are applicable to any guard, it's easier to illustrate this point with the posta corona.

To transition from a posta lunga into a posta corona, change the position of your feet so your left foot is now forward. Retract your arms so the

Crown Guard (Posta Corona)

posta corona
(PO-sta co-RO-na)

pommel is in front of your sternum. Then raise the point of your sword to a steep angle. When you do, your hands will naturally grip the hilt so the back of your hands faces your adversary. Now you are in the posta corona. If you grip the handle too tight, your elbows may face outwards, exposing your forearms to attack. Instead, keep your elbows close to your body but in front of you so that your body is protected by your forearms and your arms are protected by your quillons. To see your adversary's face, look over your quillons.

From the posta corona, you'll transition into the *posta de bicornio* or the guard of the two horns. Much like the posta lunga, the posta de bicornio helps protect you when transitioning from a low guard to high guard or vice versa. The difference between the two is the position of your hands on the hilt. In the posta lunga, your hands are extended in front of your sternum. In posta de bicornio, your hands are extended in front of whichever shoulder you prefer. (Note: This is also why it is called the guard of the two horns.) If you were to place the sword in front of your right shoulder, twist your lead hand so the back of it is angled to the ground while the fingers of the rear hand rest against the lead wrist. If you were to place the sword in front of your left shoulder, the back of your rear hand is angled up toward 11 o'clock but this time the rear hand's fingers don't rest against the lead hand wrist. These two positions makes it easier to move your sword to intercept and deflect an adversary's

Guard of the Two Horns (Posta de Bicornio)

posta de bicornio
(PO-sta day by-CORN-ee-o)

blade farther away from your body than in the posta lunga.

To transition from the posta corona into the posta de bicornio, don't change your lead foot this time. Instead, just take a step, which changes your line of attack and is the point of moving your feet with every guard transition. Technically your transition from one middle guard to another is a fendente because it lowers the tip of the sword so it points at the adversary's face. When you position your sword in front of your lead shoulder—in the picture it is the right one—your true edge faces the adversary. When you position your sword in front of your rear shoulder—in the picture, it is the left—then your false edge would face the adversary.

As I mentioned above, the middle guards—except for posta breve because of its low position—are transitional and interchangeable during a fight. What determines the guard you choose is the angle, level and distance of your adversary and his attack. If his attack comes at your head, you probably want to choose the posta corona. If the attack is coming at shoulder level, you probably want to choose posta de bicornio. If the attack is coming at your chest level, the posta lunga might be your better choice. In the end, it really depends on your ability, training and preference. This is why guards are such an important part of studying the long sword.

The High Guards

The high guards don't necessarily close a line, but they are at shoulder level or above. There are four high guards, which correspond to the four sides of your head: the front, back, right and left side. From a high guard, you can develop a lot of power because you will be bringing your sword down your shoulder to a low or middle guard. From this, it should be clear that you can only begin a fendente and end a sotani in the high guards. While it is possible to develop a lot of power with these guards, you can also move from one high guard to another high guard with a step to change your line of attack and/or make your adversary unwilling to attack you. You can also perform a thrust from the high guards by transitioning to a middle guard.

The first high guard you will learn is *posta finestra*. Its full name is actually *posta di finestra instable*, which translates to "guard of the unstable window." For the purposes of the book, I'll refer to it simply as posta finestra.

Posta finestra is the only high guard that is interchangeable with the posta lunga, posta de bicornio and posta corona because it is able to deflect

Window Guard (Posta Finestra)

posta finestra
(PO-sta fi-NES-tra)

thrusts and intercept strikes. It's position in front of your head allows you to control the adversary's blade while you step out of his line of attack and create a new line of attack for you. If the adversary is in a high guard, the posta finestra makes the adversary unable to attack. If the adversary is in a middle guard, posta finestra makes him generally unwilling to attack. If the adversary is in a low guard, the posta finestra might invite him to attack. Because of the level of your blade, it looks like you have raised a window to look at your adversary. This makes the guard unstable because it's difficult to hold your sword above your head for a long time, which

Woman's Guard (Posta di Donna)

posta di donna
(PO-sta di don-NA)

is why you'll most likely use this guard as a transition.

You'll move from the posta de bicornio, which is a middle guard, into the posta finestra. Instead of changing your lead foot this time, just take a step to the side, which changes your line of attack. This means that your left foot is still leading and your right foot is back. Also note that your lead hand is still your right hand. From the posta de bicornio, rotate your lead wrist so the top of your hand is facing upward. Then pull back your lead (right) elbow so that it's parallel with your rear shoulder and the sword is parallel with your lead shoulder. Then, raise the sword and your hands so that you create a window to look out at your adversary; your true edge faces the sky. Your "window" doesn't point at your adversary nor does it run square to your shoulders. Instead, if we return to the analogy of the clock in which your adversary is at 12, the tip of your sword is at 10 o'clock. Lifting your sword too high will open all your lines and make your arms vulnerable, Holding it too low will either leave your head unprotected or force you to duck in order to see past your sword. Also remember not to lock your wrists into position because you need them to be flexible in order to transition out of the guard.

From the posta finestra, you're going to transition into the *posta di donna* or the woman's guard. You may hear that this guard is named after Brigid, an Irish saint who was often depicted with a sword behind her head and back. I prefer the idea that the woman's guard got its name because it's sneaky. It leaves all your lines open, inviting the adversary to attack. However, the posta di donna is actually a powerful guard to develop a strike from. Because of its position, the sword fighter has a lot of space to whip his sword around, developing power for a fendente or thrust. It also hides the length of your sword from your adversary, making it difficult for him to fight to his measure and gauge his striking distance. Like the other high guards, you can also transition from the posta di donna into other guards or intercept the adversary's strike.

To transition from the posta finestra into the posta di donna, take a step back to change your line of attack. Like the posta finestra, this requires a wide stance to keep your shoulders and hips square to your adversary. Rest your weight on the lead leg in order to facilitate your eventual counterattack. Also remember to point your lead toe toward the center of your adversary. To change the position of your sword, lift it above your head and let the blade drop down behind your back. The pommel and your hands are directly next to the right side of your face. Rest the false edge of your blade on your lead (right) shoulder, angling it downward so it remains close to but doesn't touch your body. From this position, your adversary shouldn't be able to see the sword's length. Also keep your pommel elbow tucked into your chest so it's not as easy of a target; it's okay to extend your lead elbow for balance because it's not as vulnerable.

From the posta di donna, you will transition into the *posta di donna sinestra* or the woman's guard on the left. Like the posta di donna, the posta di donna sinestra positions the sword behind your head and back and is a powerful guard to develop and intercept strikes. Unlike the posta

Woman's Guard Left (Posta di Donna Sinestra)

posta di donna sinestra
(PO-sta di don-NA si-NES-tra)

di donna, the grip on the posta di donna sinestra is different; it also uses the false edge to cut instead of the true edge. This high guard is the only guard discussed in this chapter that must be done on the left side.

To transition from the posta di donna to the posta di donna sinestra, you'll first need to transition back into the posta finestra. This may seem confusing, but it will make your final guard change safer. When you're back in posta finestra, change your feet so your right foot is now forward. You want to bring the blade over your left shoulder and position it down your back. It's a very simple movement that will give you an excellent position to bring down a direct and powerful fendente. Because the grip is different in the posta di donna sinestra, lay your lead (right) thumb

Proud Woman's Guard (Pulsativa)

pulsativa
(pul-sa-tee-va)

along the flat of the sword next to your ear. Finally, if you look at the illustration, you'll notice that the sword fighter's hips look twisted. This is actually incorrect. Your shoulders and hips should directly face your adversary so that he can't see the blade at all and your sword is in the direct line of attack.

From the posta di donna sinestra, you'll transition into the *pulsativa*. The guard's full name is actually posta di donna pulsativa, which translates to "guard of the proud woman." For the purposes of the book, I'll refer to it simply as pulsativa.

Pulsativa is a variation of the woman's guard because the sword is also positioned behind your head and back. It's different because you're not facing your adversary head on. Instead, your rear-hand side faces your adversary, making you seem so proud that you don't care that all your lines are completely open. This is a misunderstood guard that is not used often because it's hard to see the benefit of the position. In reality, the pulsativa is very versatile because it allows you to immediately redirect the momentum of a sotani into a thrust. This also makes it a good guard to use to pass through and transition into other guards during a fight. However, this means that you probably shouldn't start in the pulsativa. Like other posta di donna guards, the pulsativa invites the adversary to attack.

To transition from the posta di donna sinestra into the pulsativa, you're going to transition through a few guards. First, switch back to the posta finestra by moving your left foot forward with your sword pommel on your right side. Next, regain the posta di donna. Make sure that your false edge rests on your shoulder and the blade is angled downward. To get into the pulsativa, move your right foot behind your left foot, like in the fencing stance. Then turn your body so both feet, hips and shoulders are facing the same direction but not directly at your adversary. So if your adversary is at twelve o'clock, you are facing 3 o'clock. Leaving the rest of your body at 3 o'clock, continue twisting your right foot so it points to 6 o'clock. Rest your weight on your bent right leg because this will help you guide the momentum of a sotani into a thrust position. Turn your head back to 12 o'clock so you are looking directly at your adversary.

This ends the twelve guards that are listed in Fiore dei Liberi's treatise. Now we'll move onto the 13th guard.

The 13th Guard

Unlike the other guards discussed in this chapter, this guard is from Filippo Vadi's treatise *Arte Gladiatoria*, published somewhere between 1482 and 1487. Vadi calls this guard the posta di donna, but it is different from dei Liberi's posta di donna for two reasons: Vadi's guard positions the sword in front of the body with the point facing up instead of down. To prevent confusion among my students, I call Vadi's guard the *posta falcone*. I like to think that the position of the blade in the guard rests on your shoulder like a bird of prey waiting to pounce. This is also how I will refer to this guard in this book.

The posta falcone is usually the beginning of a fendente or end of a sotani. It is a comfortable guard to hold because the sword is close to your body and there is no real stress on your arms. You can also think of this guard as a transition into or out of the posta di donna because

Guard of the Falcon (Posta Falcone)

posta falcone
(PO-sta fal-CO-nay)

you can move out of the posta di donna by sliding your hands down in front of you or end in the posta di donna by sliding your hands back. The posta falcone can make the adversary unwilling to attack or invite him to attack because the sword closes the high outside line only. Like the other guards mentioned in this chapter, you can also transition into the posta falcone from any them.

Because the posta falcone is in its own category, let's start in this guard instead of transition into it. Begin in your proper stance but with your left foot forward. Your lead hand is still the right hand. Your sword is raised, protecting your high line, and the true edge of the sword points directly at your adversary. From here, raise you quillons so they are now positioned in front but not touching your right armpit. Angle the quillons slightly toward your left side. This will also angle your true edge to the left, too. Your point will be ever so slightly angled toward and over your right shoulder. Do not allow your point to go past your right shoulder or else you expose your high outside line.

The posta falcone can only be done on the right side if your lead hand is the right hand and only be done on the left side if your lead hand is the left hand. For this example, I'll assume that your lead hand is the right hand. If you perform the posta falcone on the wrong side, your right arm will cross your chest and expose your forearm as a target.

Each guard position that you take is important. Study and practice so that you automatically assume the proper position. If you are always perfect in your guards, then this is one less thing you need to think about during your fight.

Remember, you are the most important person in your world. If you're so focused on your adversary's movements that you stop paying attention to your own, you give the adversary complete control of the fight. This is the power of knowing and using proper guards; you will never chase your adversary. Instead, you will force him to react to you.

Chapter 10:
The Path

In the previous chapter, you learned that when your feet are positioned in a certain guard, you hold your sword in a certain way. But how do you move your sword when you transition from guard to guard? It's simple: Follow the path.

The path is the route that your sword and arm travel when you move from guard to guard correctly. What makes the path work is that the motion of your sword builds momentum, guiding it around you so that you can easily change from guard to guard. Because the path is a fluid transition, trying to force a change will only strain your arms, open your lines and throw you off-balance. If you feel your arms or wrists locking into an uncomfortable position, then you've fallen off the path.

This doesn't mean, however, that the path is beaten into stone. Everyone's age, gender and history influence how they move, so my path may not be your path. While the guards are constant, the paths are individualized. This is why it's important to find the paths that work best for you.

Momentum vs. Strength

Our bodies know how to move. After all, we have been doing it all of our lives. Knowing how to move in the most natural fashion allows you to follow the path. Relying on strength to move breaks momentum, forcing your body into unnatural positions. This weakens your balance and breaks your tempo, giving control of the fight to your adversary.

This doesn't mean strength is bad. You just want to use it at the right time. Use your muscles to start the motion of your sword and the momentum of your swing. From there, your muscles guide the path but don't force the sword to move along it. The swing's natural momentum will take care of that. This allows you to conserve your energy, which is important when wielding the long sword.

Find the Path

Here's an example of a path. Use the example as a starting point to find other paths. Start in the high guard posta di donna sinestra. Your right foot is forward but your lead hand is still the right. Swing your sword down to your right side so you transition into the low guard tutta porta di ferro. How you swing your sword isn't important. Instead, focus on how the momentum of the swing carries you into the new guard. When you arrive in tutta porta di ferro, allow the momentum to carry your sword back and behind to your right shoulder, putting you in a posta di donna. From posta di donna, cut back down to your left side to arrive at a tutta porta di ferro. Your swing has created an "X."

Sample Path

Use this simple path to find other paths.

Instead of starting and stopping the sword with each guard change, continue the momentum with your first swing. You do this by "breaking" your wrist. Breaking your wrist means bending it to continue the motion and maintain the momentum of your sword. If you don't bend your wrist naturally, you will injure it, which could also allow the momentum to pull the sword out of your hand.

Forcing the Path

If you turn your wrist while moving along the path, you can hurt or disarm yourself.

Moving Your Body Around Your Sword

The path's fluidity not only depends on how you move your sword but also how you move your body around your sword. New students often forget to move their feet while transitioning from guard to guard, which is common mistake. Remember, your complete defense is one in which your footwork and sword work together. This also pertains to the path!

You need your strength and momentum to work together. When moving your body, use your hips, back and core muscles to guide your sword along the path. Don't force the sword with your body or else you may lose the path. Instead, your whole body works together so no one part is doing all the work alone.

This ability to move fluidly is also a sign that you're relaxed. If your body is tense, you wouldn't be able to move your body anyway.

Learning By The Numbers

Obviously, when you start to learn sword fighting, especially concepts like the path, you won't be able to perform the techniques fluidly. Learning by the numbers allows you to break up the actions into smaller pieces, which make them easier to understand and practice. This is useful for moving along the path because your actions don't need to be fast. Instead, they just need to be smooth. However, as you practice and improve, you'll be able to meld all those pieces into one cohesive motion. This will eventually make all your actions, defensive and offensive, less tiring and easier to execute.

Beware the trap of the numbers, though. If you try to work by the numbers in a fight, your actions and motions will most likely be rigid, tense and choppy.

Moving along the path properly is the cleanest and best way to fluidly transition between guards. Each concept in this chapter may be a part unto itself, but together they help you keep your body relaxed in combat and on the proper path.

Chapter 11:
Get a Grip

Studying the long sword is exciting, and students often get excited when practicing it. When a student gets excited, he naturally wants to tighten his grip, causing his muscles to tense.

Don't do this when you are gripping your sword. Having a stranglehold on the hilt will cause you to lose control of the blade. A tight grip tenses up your hands, arms, shoulders and neck, placing you in great danger.

As we mentioned in the previous chapter, combat requires relaxation. The ability to relax and go with the flow is the difference between a mediocre fighter and a great one. Relaxing your body begins with your grip.

The Lead Hand

The lead hand is the fulcrum point for your sword in the same way that the neck is the fulcrum point for your head. Without your neck, you would have to move your head with your shoulders. Similarly, the lead hand guides the smaller movements of the hilt, which in turn makes the larger movements of the blade.

To get the proper lead-hand grip, gingerly pinch your sword's handle with your index and thumb, as though you are touching something you don't like. Next, wrap your pinkie, ring and middle fingers around the handle. Grip the handle tightly with your pinkie, less tightly with your ring finger and even less tightly with your middle finger. This may seem difficult to do, especially in the beginning, but it gets easier with practice. Now, move your thumb so it rests on top of your middle finger. Your index finger should curl around the handle but not grip it. Because the pinkie has the tightest grip on the sword, this allows the rest of the handle to float more freely in your grip. This gives your sword mobility but not enough to cause the sword to fall out of your hands.

If you gripped the sword in a regular fist or "hammer grip," you would hold it like you would a hammer. But this means you need to use your whole arm, shoulder included, to move the sword. In the proper grip, you only need to use your wrist and forearm, taking the strain off your upper arm. In a fight, this prevents you from getting too tired and gives you more movement options.

The only variation on the proper grip that I will mention right now regards the placement of your thumb. You can place your thumb on your middle finger or you can place it on the handle, as illustrated below. Which thumb placement you choose depends on the circumstance and the action you're performing. For example, if you transition to posta finestra, the thumb on the handle helps you balance the sword over your eyes.

Proper Grip With the Lead Hand

Your grip should start from your pinkie and move up to your forefinger, gradually relaxing around your hilt.

Keeping your thumb behind your quillons protects it from attacks. If you are holding your hand tightly against your quillons and you defend against a fendente, your thumb might get hit. If you are holding your grip in the correct fashion I described, your thumb is far enough below the quillons that there is no real chance of the adversary's blade hitting your thumb.

Don't place your index finger over the quillons, because doing so leaves it totally unprotected. You run the risk of having your finger broken or cut off.

Improper Grip With the Lead Hand

If you put your index finger over the quillons, it exposes itself to a strike.

The Rear Hand

The rear hand controls the point of your sword from the pommel like a steering wheel controls the tires on a car. You can never hold your sword with just your rear hand. You need the lead hand to support the weight of the sword and direct its movements.

Place your rear hand on the pommel of the sword, gripping it as far down as you can go. Make sure there is space between your lead hand and rear hand, so you are holding the hilt like a lever and not like a baseball bat. Leave as much space as you can between your hands so both can properly grip the hilt. Generally, you want to use a loose hammerfist grip on the pommel. Don't grip it so tightly that you can't move your hand about the pommel. You could also grip it in the same fashion as the lead hand, but that depends on personal preference and whether it gives you more mobility. Always wrap your fingers around the pommel or they can become targets.

Improper Grip With the Rear Hand

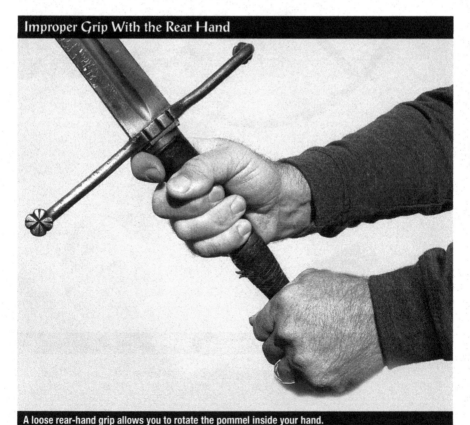

A loose rear-hand grip allows you to rotate the pommel inside your hand.

One-Handed Grip

Because the lead hand is the fulcrum of the sword, always *always* keep it on the sword in a one-handed grip. But what do you do with your rear hand? You've probably seen a sword fighter on screen who keeps his "off hand" behind the small of his back or on his hips. Practitioners of the long sword don't use these positions. Instead, keep your "off hand" relaxed against your chest and about six inches under your chin. It does not have to be right under your chin, but you do want to keep it relaxed and against your body.

There are several reasons for this. First, it keeps your adversary from easily attacking your hand. Second, it also keeps your hand out of your way while you are swinging your sword around. It is embarrassing, not to mention painful, to hit your hand with your own sword. The third reason is because your off hand is still a useful weapon if you get in close enough to grapple with your adversary's sword. (See Chapter 17.)

Using the Off Hand

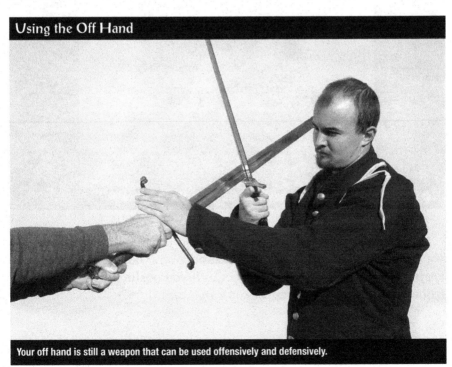

Your off hand is still a weapon that can be used offensively and defensively.

Proper Off-Hand Position When the Sword is Low

This lets you defend with your sword so you can use your off hand if you need to.

If your sword is in a low guard, you can keep your off hand around your waist level, so that you sword hides or covers your off hand. However, keep it behind your sword to protect it. If you position your off hand in front of your sword, your adversary can attack it.

Improper Off-Hand Position When the Sword is Low

Notice how the sword fighter's hand gets in the way of swinging his own sword for a counterattack.

Chapter 12:
On Offense

In the previous chapters, we learned how to position and move your sword. Now we will learn how to use that information to attack. Offense incorporates pulling on your hilt and transitioning through your guards. Your offensive actions are facilitated with your footwork. When you perform an offensive action, it can also include your defense, because every defensive action you execute can turn into an offensive action and every offensive action you execute can turn into a defensive action. Similar to how the path allows you to move your sword fluidly, your offense and defense should smoothly interchange between each other.

Don't Try To Cut Through the Adversary

An offensive action is not about swinging your sword as hard as you can; it's about getting your sword in the proper place. For example, a movie hero can often cut his adversaries in half with a powerful swing of his sword. Trying to perform these attacks in real life would cause big problems for our hero. First, if he misses, the momentum of his strike could carry his weapon off the hero's line of attack and throw his body off-balance. Second, developing a powerful swing would telegraph his

Cutting Through Scenario No. 1

When the sword fighter tries to cut through his adversary, he exposes himself to a counterattack in mezzo tempo. Note that his swing isn't even complete when the adversary intercepts his attack with a thrust.

intention to his adversary. This means that when the hero uses a big swing, the adversary can easily step aside or parry the attack, leaving our hero open to a counterattack on the mezzo tempo. Instead of trying to cut through your adversary, focus on cutting to his center mass.

Cutting Through Scenario No. 2

When the sword fighter tries to cut through his adversary, he telegraphs his intention, which allows the adversary to move off his line of attack. This causes the sword fighter to miss.

Cutting to the Center Mass

When the sword fighter cuts to the center mass, he doesn't make himself vulnerable because the tip of his sword stays between him and his adversary. Because most people will not rush toward an extended point, this gives the sword fighter the freedom to move smoothly into a defensive action regardless of whether or not he hits his target.

Three Different Kinds of Cuts

To cut to the center mass, you will use one of three body parts to power your cuts: your shoulder, elbow or wrist. Depending on how much power you need or how deep you want to cut will determine which part of the arm you use. While all three cuts are usable, knowing the differences between them will help you properly use them.

Cutting from the shoulder gives you the most power because you're able to use your entire arm and back to develop the swing. However, you will not find yourself cutting from the shoulder too often because the swing takes time to complete and telegraphs your intention, exposing you to a counterattack by your adversary. It's like trying to cut through your adversary, which is why you don't want to do it often. However, there is never a "never" or "always," which is why you want to be aware of all the strengths and weaknesses of your cuts.

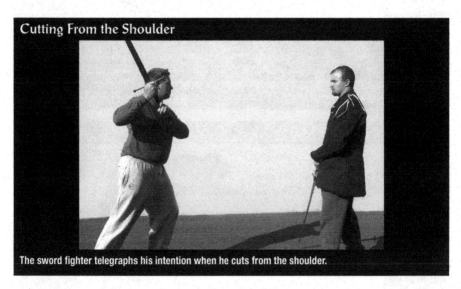

Cutting From the Shoulder

The sword fighter telegraphs his intention when he cuts from the shoulder.

Cutting from the elbow is not as dangerous as cutting from your shoulder because it doesn't telegraph your intention as much. It is easier to control the power of the cut, allowing you to stay on the path while transitioning fluidly between guards. The power of the swing is developed through your arm, which makes your attack more difficult for your adversary to read, and it allows you to keep your sword between you and your adversary.

Like the foible on the sword, cutting from the wrist is the weakest but fastest of the three cuts. It's similar to cutting from the elbow and it will be one of your primary attacks because of its speed.

Cutting From the Elbow

When cutting from the elbow, the sword fighter only uses his arm, which masks his intention and protects him from counterattacks.

Cutting From the Wrist

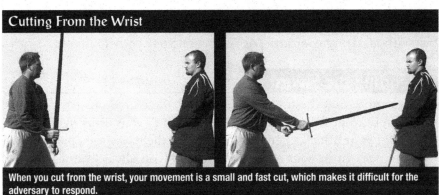

When you cut from the wrist, your movement is a small and fast cut, which makes it difficult for the adversary to respond.

Cutting from the shoulder tends to move you from a high guard to a low guard, while cutting from the elbow or wrist can be used to transition into any guard. Also note that which arm joint you cut from determines the power of your fendente, sotani or thrust.

The Pommel is Connected to the Point

Remember how the sword is a lever? When you make a small movement with the hilt, it can translate into a big movement of the point. This is how you control your cuts. How you move your pommel is directly related to where your point moves. When you push your pommel down, your point goes up. If you push your pommel up, your point will go down.

The movement of the pommel also adds to the snap of the point, which develops the force of your cut. In his treatise *His True Art of Defence* (1594), Giacomo di Grassi writes that you don't need to use a lot of physical strength to strike. In fact, you want to use less, which you do by moving

Moving the Sword With the Pommel

Notice how the sword fighter on the left doesn't have to move his arms when he attacks. Because he used the pommel, his point moved, hitting the adversary.

the pommel to move the point. This means that your strike is strong and fast without tiring your arms or relying on your body to power it.

Extending the Sword

Remember that the tip of your sword is the dangerous part, and the sweet spot is on the foible by the tip. If you pull your arms in on the execution of your attack, then you are pulling the dangerous part of your weapon away from your adversary. Instead, you always want to attack with extended arms. Extended arms help you maintain your balance, move your sword on the path and keep your point closer and between you and your adversary during a cut.

When you perform a cut, extend your arms out straight. Don't bend them and don't lock them. Straight arms just give you that extra distance

Proper Extension

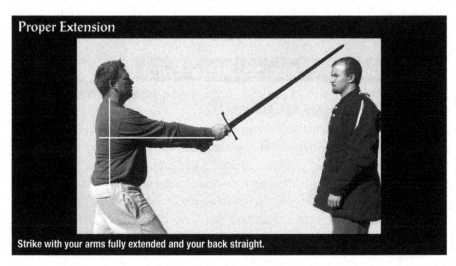

Strike with your arms fully extended and your back straight.

to make sure your cut hits your adversary. That way your body is far away from your adversary's sword, but the dangerous part of your sword is really close to him. In addition, understanding distance and measure will help your strikes be more precise.

Full arm extension also allows you to transition your offensive cut into a defensive one at the same time. Because your arms are out, your sword is too, which means that it can intercept and redirect an adversary's weapon.

The Offense in Your Hands

Back in Chapter 11, you learned that each of your hands has a specific job. These jobs affect how you extend your sword and use it for cutting.

The lead hand has two jobs: elevating the sword by moving it up and down, and extending the sword by moving it farther or closer to you. When elevating the sword, the lead hand should not be lifted above the head but only as far as necessary to transition through guards or develop a cut. When extending the sword toward the adversary, you control target measure.

The rear hand, which is sometimes called the pommel hand, has two jobs. The rear hand's job is to control the point. If you want to move the point down to cut, you pull the pommel up. If you want to move the point up to cut, you push the pommel down. Remember that you only want to use a small movement with the pommel to move the sword. If you execute a cut by punching out your lead hand, you use the strength of your arm to perform the cut. If you execute the cut by snapping the pommel, then you use the fulcrum principle discussed in Chapter 11 to develop a stronger cut while maintaining control of your blade for offense and defense.

The second job of the pommel is to provide edge control, which refers to how you angle your true edge. If you want to angle the edge to the left as in some of the middle guards, you use the rear hand to make the slight adjustment. Because this is a subtle movement, the handle of the sword will rotate slightly in your lead hand, so don't try and perform edge control with the lead hand. If you do, the lead wrist could bend awkwardly.

Snap the pommel when your arms are fully extended to strengthen your attack. You do this for any attack (fendente, sotani or thrust) launched from any location (shoulder, elbow or wrist). At the moment your arms are extended, it is easier to manipulate the point of the sword with the pommel because you have gravity on your side. As always, any movement of the sword should actually be a transition from guard to guard.

For example, you are in the middle guard posta breve so that the sword is extended in front of you and pointed at your adversary's face. Attack his head or shoulders by extending your arms straight. Pull up on the pommel so your point drops, allowing you to cut from the wrist. This is not a strong cut but it is fast.

You can also use your rear hand to move the pommel and point from side to side. If you pull the pommel to the left, the point will move to the right, and if you pull the pommel to the right, the point will move to the left.

You can also manipulate the pommel and point for defense. For example, if an adversary attacks you, you only have to move your pommel so that your blade will block or parry the attack. It's also useful to know when practicing with training partners. Because you don't want to hurt your training partner, you can manipulate the blade to transition your offensive action into a defensive one or out of your line of attack. For instance, if you execute a fendente from a high guard but notice it may hit your training partner on his bare neck, you pull your pommel up just a little bit so your target shifts from the neck to your partner's shoulder. With just a little movement, you and your friend can avoid a very bad situation.

To Step or Not to Step

The footwork you choose to combine with your cuts affects how far you can extend. If you move your whole body toward your adversary, you may be too close to hit the target with your sweet spot. Also, if you move into your adversary and do not have control of his weapon, then he can move out of your line of attack and execute a counterattack.

Stepping in Too Close

If you step too close to you adversary, you may hit him with your forte instead of your sweet spot.

If you step in too close to your adversary, he may be able to block the attack with his sword or even his free arm.

The Dynamic Fight

Remember, sword fighting is dynamic, not static. Think of it as a lively debate. If one debater is screaming, he may not hear the important part of the other's argument. In the case of sword fighting, the screaming debater probably doesn't know what's going on, whereas you will know how to give the proper response because you listened. If you don't know what your adversary is doing, how will you execute the right action that will keep you safe? That's why a sword fight is a lively debate—there is give and take. Both sword fighters try to react with the proper response in order to control and force their adversary to concede defeat.

Chapter 13:
Drills

The drills in this chapter build on concepts you learned in Section I and Section II.

Drills for Stance

No. 1: Leaning in or bending at the waist (see Chapter 3) moves your head closer to your adversary's sword and leaves you vulnerable to a counterattack. Doing so also places your center of gravity in front of your feet, sabotaging your own balance and limiting the ways you can move.

Try this experiment. Lean forward, then move your body back quickly, keeping your feet planted as if someone is swinging a sword at you. Notice how this action takes too long and probably will get you hit. It also throws you off-balance. If you try to avoid the hit by stepping back, you will still be vulnerable to an attack because your upper body is still extended. If you try to step back and swing your upper body back, then you will be even more seriously off-balance.

Instead, stand with your feet in a proper stance and extend your arms and hands in front of you as if you are striking. (If it's easier for you, stand in a posta lunga.) Your center of gravity is over your hips, and you will use proper footwork and bend your knees to avoid a strike. Step back as if you are avoiding a swing. You will find that you are able to move much quicker, maintain your balance and not present an easy target for your adversary.

No. 2: In this drill, you will learn to be aware of the adversary's balance and take advantage of it if he isn't moving correctly.

Face your training partner directly. He will stand with his right foot forward and his left arm extended forward. This is an obvious sign that he doesn't have four legs and his balance is weak. Push your training partner's left elbow across to his right side. Because he has no leg underneath to support his left arm, his body is already twisted, and your push takes advantage of his mistake. Combat of any kind always comes down to training, distance and balance. By working on these three elements, you gain the advantage over your adversary.

Drill to Develop Peripheral Vision

No. 1: A good way to develop peripheral vision is to work with your training partner. Assume any guard position across from your training partner. Have him move his sword slowly along the path, transitioning from guard to guard. Look at his chest but don't focus on it. In your peripheral vision, you should be able to see his head, and both of his arms, and be aware when his shoulders, his legs and feet move. From the movement of his shoulders and other body parts, you should be able to point out the location of his sword.

Throughout this entire drill, there is no contact between your adversary and your sword. You are learning to "see" your adversary and the surroundings.

Visual Aid for Peripheral-Vision Drill No. 1

While your training partner transitions from guard to guard, locate his sword with just your peripheral vision.

Drills for Measure

Distance is not an easy concept to understand. In fact, it is one of the more difficult concepts to understand in sword fighting. To correctly apply this concept to combat, you must practice constantly, so here are three drills.

No. 1: Stand in front of your training partner. Raise your right arm, and have your partner mirror you so that your fingertips touch. This is the measure you want for this drill. When you have it, both of you will drop your arms back to your right sides.

Then, like in dancing, one of you will "lead" and one will "follow." The follower will follow the movements of the leader while trying to maintain that measure. The leader can move in any direction he wants. For example, if the leader takes a step back, the follower takes a step forward. Periodically, the leader will raise his right arm so that the follower can check and see if the measure is still correct. Note: This is just an introduction to distance. Mimicking your adversary's movements is not something you would do during combat.

No. 2: Stand in front of your training partner with your practice swords or swordlike objects. Raise your swords so that your sweet spots are resting on the other's shoulder. This is "sword distance." When you have this measure, drop your swords back to your sides, as though you were placing them in your respective scabbards. Once again, one person will lead and the other will follow. The leader begins walking while the other maintains the sword measure. The leader wanders in any direction and will periodically take out his sword to see if you have maintained your distance properly.

Visual Aid for Measure Drill No. 3

Your adversary executes a fendente.

By stepping back, you avoid his attack.

Even though you are safe from his attack, you now have the option to hit him.

No. 3: This drill involves swinging your sword at your partner. Do not swing it fast or hard. Practice carefully.

Your partner will execute a fendente on you. To get the proper distance, he rests his sweet spot on your shoulder like in drill No. 2. He then steps back, changing his lead foot. Slowly, he will swing his sword from a high guard, cutting from his shoulder and stepping forward. As the swing comes in, move your lead foot back so that it is even with your rear foot, but not so much that you are in horse stance or lose your balance. That takes your body out of the reach of the fendente, keeping you safe.

Drills for Tempo

Here are some drills for you to practice to learn how to use timing to your advantage.

No. 1: Both you and your training partner should choose any guard. It does not matter whether it is a high, low or middle guard. Your training partner will transition into another guard; again it doesn't matter which one. As he begins to transition, you will "attack" the closest target. This drill will help you identify when your adversary's balance is shifting and an opening is available.

Visual Aid for Tempo Drill No. 1

While your training partner transitions from guard to guard, locate his sword with just your peripheral vision.

No. 2: Once again, your training partner and you can choose any guard. In this drill, you both will take turns as the attacker. This is much like the measure drills, except you will be using footwork as well. Don't concentrate on maintaining distance because you're practicing tempo. If you notice your training partner's balance shift, such as when he moves in a different direction, that is when you want to time your attack.

Drills for Pulling Your Hilt

These drills will help you to learn to pull your hilt as you are transitioning between guards.

No. 1: Stand facing your training partner. Both partners should start in the posta breve and be out of both striking and cutting distance. Pull your hilt back to your hip. This should naturally raise the point of your sword, closing your high line. If you pull to your lead-hand hip, you close your outside line. If you pull it to your rear-hand hip, you close your inside line. While you do this, your training partner is watching to ensure that when you pull the hilt, the blade doesn't swing so wide that it leaves all your lines open.

No. 2: This is a continuation of the first drill. You are standing with your hilt on your lead-hand hip, and your outside line is closed. You and your partner are still in posta breve. Now, your training partner will slowly swing, targeting the shoulder of your inside line. Defend this attack with a parry. Remember, you are both friends. He shouldn't swing so hard or fast that he puts you in danger or vice versa. As he swings, pull your hilt across and back to your inside-line hip. When you pull the hilt out, your forte catches his foible. Then, when you pull the hilt into your inside-line hip, it redirects the energy of his swing, parrying your training partner's sword out and away from your body.

No. 3: This is a cutting drill for pulling the hilt. You will stand in a high guard. Your training partner will stand with his sword extended in front and perpendicular to your body so you can use it as a target. He stands far enough away that when you step and lower your sword, your sweet spot strikes his mezza.

Cut from your elbow with a fendente so that you hit his mezza. Then pull your hilt so that you can perform a slicing action. If you don't pull from your hilt, you just end up bashing his sword straight down.

Drills for Pushing Your Hilt

Here are two drills that you can use with your partner to help you become comfortable pushing your hilt to defend yourself.

No. 1: You and your partner are facing each other and standing at a distance in which you can hit each other's shoulder with your sweet spot by stepping. You are standing in the low guard mezza porta di ferro, and he is standing in the high guard posta di donna.

Your training partner will step forward and slowly cut from his shoulder to your shoulder with a fendente. You will lift your hilt and tap his mezza on your mezza as you transition into the posta falcone. This will redirect the path of his sword so that he completely misses your shoulder. Remember to be careful when you swing your swords—safety first!

Visual Aid for Pushing-Your-Hilt Drill No. 1

Catch your training partner's mezza on your mezza, then push the hilt.

No. 2: This drill is the same as the first but with footwork. Your training partner performs a fendente, targeting your shoulder. As you transition from your low guard to a high guard, you will step toward your inside line while pushing your hilt. By combining footwork with pushing the hilt, you redirect his sword even farther.

Section III

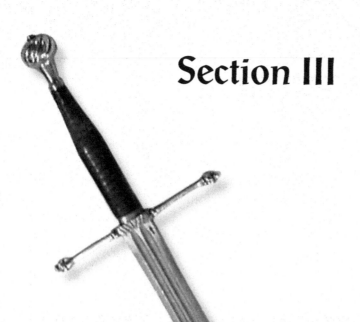

Become a True Beginner
With More Study

Note to Reader:

In the third section, we explore concepts, principles and drills in greater depth. It adds more drills, revisits terms and looks at underlying principles that make these drills work. In the end, this section provides insights into the limitations of this book. I hope you use this information to continue your studies in greater depth and safety with a school or group.

Chapter 14:
Basic Parry

As we discussed in Chapter 8, a parry redirects the adversary's power so that you don't have to pit your strength against his. Parrying can also be used to create opportunities to counterattack. There are many ways to parry, but our focus is the basic parry. It is called the basic parry because it is a defensive movement that becomes second nature with practice. If someone asks you what 2+2 equals, do you need to even think about the answer? No. You know the answer is four because you practiced it thousands of times in school. The basic parry is like that. After learning how to parry, you won't have to waste precious seconds thinking about how to defend yourself when you are in an "oh crap" defense situation.

Whenever you intend to use a basic parry, you will execute it from the middle guard posta breve.

The Problem with "V"

The basic parry can take two forms: the "V" and the "A." The "V" is the natural movement while the "A" is a trained movement.

It's called the "V" because your point to your pommel will write out a letter "V" when you parry. It's like a windshield wiper. When a wiper moves across the windshield, the base is stationary, and the tip of it moves from side to side.

People are naturally inclined to parry with this movement because it feels strong. When in a sword fight, you need to react quickly to an incoming attack because you don't have time to think when an adversary's sword is coming at you. The "V" feels very proactive. It moves out to intercept the adversary's blade so that you can push it away and keep it as far away from you as possible.

Even though the "V" feels natural, it is dangerous to do. When you parry, you want to redirect your adversary's strike out and away from you. But the "V" doesn't do that. Instead it causes the adversary's blade to do one of three things:

1. The "V" depends on the movement of the wrist, which means pitting your wrist strength against the strength of the adversary's cut, momentum and body weight. Because these three things added together are always stronger than the pushing of your wrist, your

adversary may be able to force his blade and your blade into you. In this scenario, you're not only struck by your adversary but by your own sword, too.

2. When parrying with the "V," you push out with the weakest part of the blade (the foible) to redirect your adversary's weapon. At the same time, you keep the most defensive parts (the forte and the hilt) in front and close to your body but far away from your adversary's sword. It is dangerous because the momentum of the adversary's cut will follow the path of least resistance, which is right down your sword blade. In this scenario, you stop your adversary's attack on your sword but allow his sword to slide down, hitting your hands or arms.

3. You're successful! You bounce his blade off of yours, parrying it outside of your body lines.

As you can see, your chances of safely redirecting an attack with the "V" are poor and your safety is never worth the risk. Even if you do manage to successfully parry the attack with a "V," your blade is now out of position and off your line of attack, leaving you unable to defend against counterattacks.

Basic "V" Movement

Pushing your point while keeping your hands in front of you creates a "V" movement with your sword.

What this means is that you will have very little protection between your hands and your adversary's blade when it slides down. The "V" parry leaves your arm and chest vulnerable to a cut or thrust respectively.

Sliding Your Sword Down the Blade, No. 1

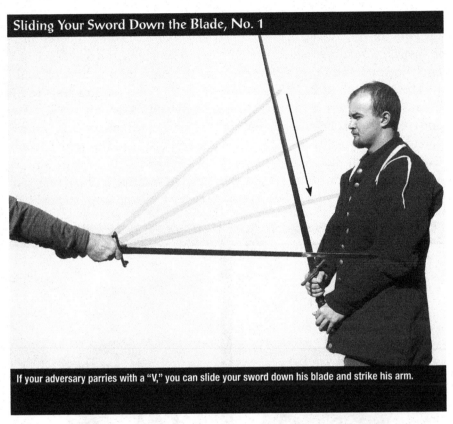

If your adversary parries with a "V," you can slide your sword down his blade and strike his arm.

Sliding Your Sword Down the Blade, No. 2

If your adversary parries with a "V," you can slide your blade down his sword, run over his quillons with a little force, and strike his lead forearm.

When you strike his forearm, you actually want to thrust behind it.

The Benefits of an "A"

You want to execute the basic parry with the trained movement or the "A."

In the "A," you use the hilt to parry instead of the point. Imagine that the point of your sword is chained to the ceiling and you can never move it. Instead, you move the hilt from hip to hip depending on which side you are being attacked from. This creates an "A" shape for you to parry with.

The reason that the "A" is a trained instead of a natural response is because you keep your hilt close to your body and your point in place. You don't reach, push or thrust anything out to stop an incoming attack. Instead, you trust your position to redirect his power away from you, which it will. Even if your adversary slides his sword down your blade, he can't hit you. This is because your hilt is positioned outside your hips, protecting your lines. In addition, your hands are protected by the quillons, so his blade

General "A" Position

From the left side, pull the hilt down to your hip without moving your hands away from your body.

Whenever you assume the "A" basic-parry position, the lead-hand wrist should be straight; it shouldn't be bent awkwardly. This allows you to pull your hilt farther down your hip without dropping your shoulder or bending your back to better protect your hands. Otherwise, you hold the sword in the same position on your left hip.

will slide to the outside of your body. You are as safe as you can be for a person in a sword fight.

When you pull your hilt to your hip, keep your point upright so that the foible is not extended forward. If your point is leaning toward the adversary, your foible can be hit by the mezza or forte of the incoming blade. If your adversary catches your foible, he will be able to go right though your defense because it is the weakest part of your blade.

By keeping your point up, you also enhance your ability to counterattack the adversary. When the force of his cut hits your quillons, it can move your point from an upright position to a more forward position, so you can now thrust.

Basic Parry With a Counterattack

When doing a basic parry, you can counterattack with a thrust.

Chapter 15:
Cuts

So far, you've learned how to perform a fendente, sotani and thrust as well as how to cut from the shoulder, elbow and wrist. You've also seen how to cut when transitioning from guard to guard. In this chapter, we're going to take a more in-depth look at the cuts available to you, specifically some variations on the fendente and sotani as well as cuts to the middle guards.

Contracting Guards

In Chapter 12, you learned that it's important to extend your arms when you cut because cutting with your sword is a matter of contraction and expansion. Extending your arms delivers a cut, then contracting them pulls your hilt to develop power and control the cut. Never cut with a smashing action. Instead, cut with a slicing action. No matter which guard you cut from, always extend and contract.

There are some guards that are naturally contracted. These guards start close to your body, so you need to extend your arms out when you transition. During the transition, you naturally contract your arms to get into a new guard. The posta di donna, posta di donna sinestra and pulsativa are all examples of contracted guards.

If there are contracted guards, it's reasonable to assume that there are extended guards. These guards don't start close to the body, so you won't be able to just extend and cut. Instead, you need to contract the sword and then extend it with your arms to deliver a cut. You finish the motion by contracting your arms again to slice your target. Think of the coda lunga, which is an extended low guard. The coda lunga starts out behind your body. To attack your adversary, you can't just swing the blade around your body like Conan the Barbarian. You need to make contracted and extended movements to move your blade along the path to deliver a cut.

The following is an example that will illustrate how you perform an extend-and-contract cut by transitioning guards:

Cutting With Power

You want to cut at your adversary but you can't because your arms are extended down in the middle guard of posta breve. Before attacking, you need to develop power for your cut.

To develop power, contract your position by transitioning into the high guard of posta finestra.

From posta finestra, snap back into the middle guard of posta lunga, cutting from the elbow.

Always move your sword before closing the distance with your body, so your sword is always in front of you for protection. Also, time your attack so that the foot you're stepping with lands at the same time as your cut.

Ascending and Descending Cuts

In this section, I am going to assume that you are right handed. Remember, you are the most important person in the world when you are practicing or in a sword fight. In this book, and in your training, all the cuts and transitions you do are from your perspective. When discussing cuts, when I say from the right, I mean your right or dominate side. Practice your cuts in a mirror or with a partner. When with a partner, don't hit him. Instead, use him as a target reference.

When you perform a cut, you can execute it from either side. If you cut from your right side, the attack is a fendente or sotani and strikes with your true edge. If you cut from your left side, the attack is a *fendente sinestra* or *sotani sinestra* and strikes with your false edge. *Sinestra* is the Medieval Italian word for "left." In this book, I will denote any attack from your left side with that word.

The fendente and fendente sinestra are descending blows that following a sharp and downward trajectory from a high guard to a low guard. The trajectory is important because it makes the cut both an offensive and defensive move. The cut is offensive because it attacks the adversary but defensive because it keeps the sword between you and your adversary. While the trajectory is important, the target is not. As long as you follow the path of your trajectory, you can target the adversary's head, shoulder, arms or ribs. This trajectory also means that even if you parry or block your adversary's sword, you have still performed a fendente.

Path of the Fendente

The trajectory that you follow for a *fendente* is along the adversary's left eye to his right knee with your true edge. This doesn't mean you cut through him. Instead, this is your descending path.

Fendente Sinestra

The trajectory that you follow for a fendente sinestra is along the adversary's right eye to his left knee with your false edge. This doesn't mean you cut through him. Instead, this is your descending path.

The sotani and the sotani sinestra are ascending cuts that follow a sharp upward trajectory from a low guard to a high guard. Like a fendente, while the trajectory is very important in this cut, the target is not as important. You can perform a sotani at the adversary's knee, thigh, hip, ribs or the side of the head. As long as you follow the proper trajectory, you have performed a sotani and you will be able to intercept the adversary's sword if he attacks you. Both ascending cuts are also defensive and offensive actions.

Path of the Sotani

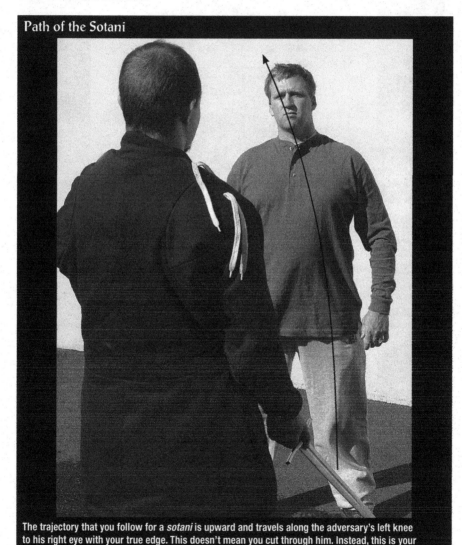

The trajectory that you follow for a *sotani* is upward and travels along the adversary's left knee to his right eye with your true edge. This doesn't mean you cut through him. Instead, this is your ascending path.

Path of the Sotani Sinestra

The trajectory that you follow for a *sotani sinestra* is upward and travels along the adversary's right knee to his left eye with your false edge. This doesn't mean you cut through him. Instead, this is your ascending path.

The next cut is the *mezzana*, which is both an ascending and descending cut. There is no "right" or "left" for this cut. Instead, think of the mezzana as a half cut. You execute them following the same trajectory as you would for a fendente or sotani. The difference is that you cut to a middle guard. When you execute a fendente or sotani, you cut from a high guard to low guard or a low guard to high guard. But when you execute a mezzana, you intentionally transition from a high guard to a middle guard or a low guard to a middle guard to attack.

Like any cut, the trajectory you follow for the mezzana is more important than the target you hit. The mezzana can strike the head, face, shoulders or arms. You cut with the true edge when you attack from your right side and you cut with the false edge when you attack from your left side.

As a general rule, perform cuts from the right with a true edge and cuts from the left with a false edge. This rule isn't concrete, so you can switch, but this topic is extremely complicated. I recommend that you try cutting from your left and right side so you understand where your edges are when you move your sword. Also look into branching out and studying with a teacher or group.

Descending Mezzana

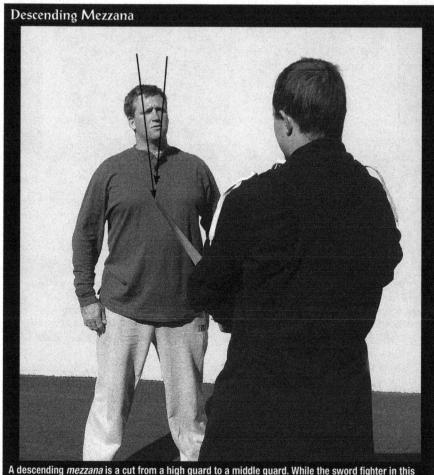

A descending *mezzana* is a cut from a high guard to a middle guard. While the sword fighter in this illustration cuts from the right with his true edge, you can execute a descending mezzana on your left or right side.

Ascending Mezzana

Even though you can execute an ascending *mezzana* from your left or right side, in this picture, the sword fighter cuts from his left side with his false edge.

The Thrust

Besides the six cuts you just learned, you also can thrust. The thrust—which is called the *punte* in Italian—transitions from a contracted guard to an extended guard on a linear path. You can thrust to the body or the head. While a thrust to the leg is possible, it is very dangerous because your sword is low and your head is exposed. You generally want to transition into a middle guard to thrust because that's when the sword is extended in front of you. For example, you can transition from the low guard mezza porta di ferro into the middle guard posta breve to thrust. You can also transition from a high guard like the posta finestra into a middle guard like the posta lunga to thrust. Or you can transition from a middle guard like the posta breve into a middle guard like the posta lunga to a thrust; in posta breve, your hands are contracted, but in posta lunga, your hands are extended. These are a few of the thrusts available to you. Have fun experimenting with the transitions to find which are the most effective for thrusts.

Unlike cuts, extension and contraction are not as important for thrusts because they can use your footwork to power the linear action.

This means that you can also perform a thrust from a fully extended middle guard, like the posta lunga or posta de bicornio, by just stepping forward. You can also perform a thrust when executing a basic parry.

Thrust

This is a thrust from the low guard of *denti di cinghiale* into a *posta lunga.*

Chapter 16:
Being in the Center

Lines of attack are the lines that you use to attack your adversary. There are weak lines of attack and strong lines of attack. On a weak line of attack, your hands and sword are not in front of your body. This lengthens measure to the target and shortchanges your attack strength because you are powering your swing with only your arms. On a strong line of attack, your hands and sword are in front of your body, shortening measure and powering your swing with your arms, body and footwork.

The ideal line of attack is the center line. You always want to attack your adversary on your center line, and he always wants to position you in his center line. Because you and your adversary are both trying to manipulate each other into an ideal line of attack, you need to think of the center line in two ways. First, the center line is your line of attack. Second, the center line is his line of attack.

Your Center Line

Your center line begins with you being in the proper stance because it is the platform from which you launch attacks and move. The guards you transition through also affect your center line. Remember, as you move through a fight from guard to guard, you want to position your feet and sword in a certain way to get your best line of attack, which is your center line. When you are taking the center line in this way, you need to keep your hips square to your adversary. This hip positioning allows you freedom of movement, and it also puts more strength behind your strikes because you are able to power your cut with your whole body. Understanding that you want to keep your hips facing your adversary is simple on the intellectual level but much more difficult do it when you are moving. (Note: Remember how some guards, like denti di cinghiale, had wider stances? It is to keep your hips square to your adversary.)

Here is a drill to help you learn how to keep your hips square and in the proper stance as you move:

Drill No. 1: Movement

You and your training partner should assume the proper stance. Your swords can overlap, but you want to be far enough away that you don't accidentally step into each other's points. Each of you should put the pommel of your own sword on your navel and extend the blade out to point where your hips are aimed. Because you are facing your training partner squarely, you have a center line of attack.

Maintain a center line of attack while moving. Keeping the pommel on your navel and your sword extended, step to the side while your training partner remains stationary. If you have maintained the center line, your hips, sword and stance will be angled but remain square to your adversary. If you are off the center line, your hips, sword and stance won't be square to your adversary; they will point somewhere else.

You'll notice in the drill that you need to angle your body and sword when stepping to the side to maintain a center line of attack and proper stance. Angles make it easier for you to attack your adversary while making it difficult for him to defend. When you take an angle with your footwork, you move your center line, but your adversary doesn't move his. This means that he doesn't have a direct line of attack on you. To regain his center line, he must turn to face you by transitioning defensively into another guard.

The angle that you take depends on which guard you need to transition into in order to place your hips and stance square to your adversary. It also limits the guards he can transition into because certain guards may actually give you more targets to hit. For example, like in the drill, you step to the side, maintaining a center line of attack. Your adversary is consequently left in a middle-guard position and off his center line of attack. As he tries to realign on you and change to a high or middle guard, he could expose one of his arms as a target for a cut or thrust. Simply put, using angles properly can give you more options for attacks.

In the following sequences, you'll see how to combine footwork with angles to gain the advantage of your center line. If you decide to practice this footwork with a partner, stop periodically to check and make sure your hips are still squared to him.

Traverse Step

To perform a traverse step, simply step out of your adversary's line of attack to the left or right side. When you traverse, you actually widen the distance between you and him.

Even though you step in a straight line away from you adversary, keep your hips and center line on him.

Slope Step Forward

The slope step is a forward right or forward left step that closes measure on a new center line. When you slope step, move the foot that corresponds to the direction you are moving; that foot also becomes or maintains the lead position. In this picture, the sword fighter is leading with the left foot but wants to slope step to the right.

The sword fighter steps forward and to the right with his right foot, changing his lead leg. If he wanted to slope step to the left, he would step forward and to the left with his left foot, keeping it as his lead. As always, he ends in a good stance. (Note: You can slope step back. It is just the reverse of the slope step forward, except that it elongates measure on a new center line.)

Circle Step

The circle step is similar to the slope step. You move the foot that corresponds to the direction you are moving, you change or maintain the lead foot depending on the direction. The circle step changes your angle but maintains the measure, so you never move closer or farther away from your adversary. Like the diameter of a circle, you are always at the same distance.

Performing the circle step to the left or right will allow you to move around your adversary so that you can create a new center line.

When you move, you want to change your center line, angle and distance to stay out of your adversary's center line. Keep your movements small so that you don't lose tempo but large enough to change your center line. How large or small you step depends on the individual because each person has a different build and stride. However, don't take giant steps. Giant steps don't change your line faster. In fact, they hurt your balance and stance because they move your shoulders over your hips and slow you down. This also exposes more targets to your adversary.

If you have not changed your center line, the most dangerous directions to move are straight forward and straight back. If you move straight forward, you run the risk of running into your adversary's sword because he can transition into a middle guard to cut with a mezzana. The danger of moving straight back is twofold. First, you cannot see what is behind you. If you walk into something, you can easily trip and fall. Second, it's easier and faster for your adversary to move forward than it is for you to move backward. Basically, moving forward or backward doesn't change your center line and prevents you from gaining the advantage over your opponent.

The Adversary's Center Line

To get your center line of attack, sometimes you need to control and redirect your adversary's sword. To do that, you need to use tempo and your knowledge of the blade.

Even though you learned three different kinds of tempo, you most likely want to use stesso tempo to control your adversary's center line. Remember that stesso tempo is when you counterattack to protect yourself; you defend with an offensive action when your adversary is in midattack. Moreso than the other tempos, stesso tempo allows you to hit your adversary and throw off his line of attack while avoiding being hit with a single movement. Also, because you catch your adversary's sword in midattack, the force of your two blades meeting will automatically throw off his line. This means that you're in the center line that you want, while your adversary must recover and move his sword back to his center line.

Be careful that you don't launch your counterattack too early or too late. When cutting into your adversary's attack, you want his foible to be close enough to intercept with your mezza. Because the foible is the weakest part of his blade, it's easier to redirect the entire sword with the mezza, which is the stronger part on your blade. If you move too soon, you can intercept his mezza with your foible. From there, it's easier for your adversary to redirect your blade and do the exact opposite of what you want, which is controlling your center line. If you move too late, you get hit. You also want to make sure that you catch his sword on the inside line because you want to redirect the adversary's sword to his outside line, making it more difficult for him to recover his center line.

To practice controlling the adversary's center line, here are two drills.

In the first drill, your training partner stands with his sword in the high line as if he is in the process of doing a fendente. Your job is to start in posta falcone and cut a fendente without stepping. Note: You and your training partner should be far enough away from each other so that when you slide down his sword with your sword, you don't hit his head or hands.

Because of your distance, your foible will intercept his static foible. Your foible will slide down his blade and move it out of position as you complete the fendente and take the center line. Do not "beat" his sword out of the way. Instead, follow the proper trajectory of a fendente to redirect his sword.

The second drill is similar to the first except that you and your training partner will stand closer together, so that when you strike at his sword, you will hit his forearms. Your training partner will slowly cut with a fendente at you. Because your training partner won't be static, be extra careful when performing this drill. Remember, you are both friends, and neither of you needs to try to knock the other's head off.

Slowly have your training partner cut at you from the elbow with a fendente. Without moving your feet, you cut in with a fendente so it intercepts his attack on stesso tempo. You are practicing timing in this drill, which is why you don't need to worry about your feet.

Why Feint?

Another way you can control an adversary's center line is by feinting. When I say feinting, I don't mean that a person passes out. Instead, what I'm referring to is a "false play."

The 19th century sword master John Taylor described a feint as "an offer at a cut or thrust without striking home. The purpose of feints being only to induce your adversary to guard a part at which you do not design to strike." When you feint, you perform an attack that you expect your adversary to defend against. Because you change your center line and attack the adversary's open line, he must defend himself or move out of the way. However, while you're prepared for his movement, he's not prepared for your sudden change to another line of attack.

In the end, you use feints to change your center line and keep the adversary off his. Using tempo, footwork and measure, the adversary constantly second guesses your intention. Because your feint changes center lines, make sure that you don't fall off the path. If you do, you will put more strain on your arms and body, which will slow down your actions enough that your adversary will recover his center line. If you follow the path, correctly change your guards, maintain tempo and measure, you will maintain your center line while putting your adversary off his in such a way that he won't be able to defend himself from your attacks. Do not rely on feints as your catchall technique. The feint is a tool in your arsenal, but use it sparingly or your adversary may be able to read your patterns and your feint can become your downfall.

Don't Rush To Get Into the Fight

Think of your center line as the compass of your fight. You always want it to point "north," which is when your hips are squared directly to your adversary. This is why you don't want to rush in. If you do, you're not paying attention to how your center line is oriented to your adversary, which means that you aren't in control of yourself. At the same time, you don't want to roam in a fight. If you do, your excessive movement gives your adversary the opportunity to take over the tempo of your movement to attack you.

If you are going to move, then move for a reason. Also, be ready to move in any direction and angle that the situation calls for. Use your movement to close distance, open distance, go left or right, and to take away your adversary's options and advantages of the center line.

Chapter 17:
Closing the Distance

You should never close the distance with your adversary unless you have a plan. If you do close without a plan, you give the adversary the opportunity to control the terms of the fight. Who do you think will win? And do you want to risk that?

At the same time, never close the distance unless you have control of the adversary's weapon because you run the risk of getting hit before you can do something to him, as you learned in the previous chapter.

When you do close, you also have the opportunity to control your adversary's sword with your hands. To do so, you must be in a position that makes him unable to use his sword offensively. In this chapter, you'll look at some of the ways this can be done.

Two Points of Contact on the Sword

To prevent your adversary from using his sword offensively, you need to stop the momentum of his weapon through guard transitions or blocking. What you're trying to do is stop his foible or mezza on your forte. From here, you will use the principle of two points of contact to make sure he can't do anything else.

To use the principle of two points of contact, grip your adversary's mezza with your rear hand and place your forearm on your adversary's foible. (Remember your lead hand never lets go of your own weapon) Technically, you grip the adversary's mezza on the flat; your fingers are on one side and your thumb is on the other. Don't wrap your hand around his sword in a fist, but you do want the adversary's mezza to press into your palm. You know you have the correct hold on his weapon when the flat of his blade is resting on the underside of your forearm arm.

Proper Grip

The sword fighter grips the adversary's mezza and foible with the proper two points of contact. His grip is also correct.

Improper Grip

Notice how the sword fighter's hand is gripping the sword edges. If the adversary pulls his blade free, he will be cut.

By controlling the sword with the proper grip, you're able to use your arm as a lever. Push down with you rear elbow and flex with your wrist. This will bend—yes, it will actually bend—the blade, preventing the adversary from pulling it straight out of your grip and cutting your hand. It's not a large bend but it will give you enough leverage to control the blade and throw off the adversary's tempo. Note: You can't hold it there indefinitely.

Bending the Sword

Notice how the sword bends. The adversary can't pull it out of the sword fighter's hand.

Another way to grip the blade is from underneath. To do so, grip the blade with the thumb and heel of your hand on the flat—your thumb should be facing down—and with your fingers on the top of the blade. The two points of contact are a bit different; this time the first point is where your hand grips the adversary's mezza or foible while the second point is where the adversary's blade rests on your quillons.

This grip is not as powerful as the first because it's easier for your adversary to pull his sword out and away. Instead, this grip is meant to delay your adversary long enough for you to cut or stab him.

Proper Grip No. 2

Point One

Point Two

To lock the adversary's blade in place, the sword fighter pulls his hand down to bend it slightly.

Here's a drill so you can practice two points of contact with grips. While your training partner stands in the middle guard of posta lunga, face him in the low guard mezza porta di ferro. You are both in thrusting distance if you step forward. Be careful that you don't actually stab your training partner!

Your training partner steps forward to simulate a chest-level thrust. You counter his attack by transitioning into the middle guard posta corona to intercept his blade. Make sure your lead hand and foot are forward.

Catch his foible or mezza on your quillons in midtransition. This means that you finish in posta corona with his point above your head and caught on your quillons. As you raise his point above your head, release your rear hand from the pommel and grip his blade from below about seven inches in front of your quillons. Don't grab too closely to where the blades cross or else your fingers might get scissored between them.

To grip it from above, take his sword outside your body, so you can reach over and grab it from the top.

Controlling His Hilt with Your Hand

Taking control of the adversary's hilt gives you two options. First, you can hold his sword and hands in place while you hit him with your own sword or kick him in the knees with your legs. Second, you can disarm him.

The difference between controlling the blade and controlling the hilt depends on how deep you step in and close the distance. As you take control of his weapon, you can choose to move in close enough to manipulate his hilt and hands. This gives you better control of his weapon because you are controlling the parts that are closest to him and limiting his ability to use and move his sword. Remember you will never want to step into your adversary unless you have control of his weapon, or you run a great risk of getting hit before you can do something to him.

Here are two drills that demonstrate how to control the hilt.

For the first drill, stand in the low guard mezza porta di ferro while your training partner stands in the middle guard posta lunga. You are both standing at a distance where you could hit each other with a thrust if you stepped forward. Remember not to actually stab your partner!

Have your training partner slowly thrust toward your chest. To defend against his attack, transition into the middle guard of posta breve and execute a basic parry to your inside line. As you defend, step forward with your rear-hand foot, closing the distance deeply. Release your rear hand from your pommel and reach over your lead arm so you can grip your training partner's hilt.

This grip on the hilt also gives you two points of contact—your hand is on his hilt and your forte is touching his mezza. Pull your training partner's hilt toward your high outside line and simulate a cut with a

Gripping the Hilt

Point One

Point Two

The sword fighter reaches over his lead hand to grip his adversary's hilt.

fendente sinestra by pushing down through his mezza. Remember to move with your attack to put power behind your strike.

In the second drill, you will disarm your training partner. Reposition yourselves in the same guards like in the first drill. Your training partner thrusts again, then you counter with a basic parry to the inside line while transitioning into a posta breve.

When you parry, close the distance so you can reach your training partner's hilt in the proper rear-hand grip. Once you have it, step straight back with your lead foot, while holding onto his hilt, and pull it toward your lead-hand shoulder. By combining the strength of your grip, body and step, you will be able to pull his sword out of his grip.

Remember to control the adversary's weapon before you close distance. After all, you're the one who is ultimately responsible for your safety. Don't rush in and hope something works; have a plan when you close.

Nay More:
Conclusion

Here I end my first book. While I have only covered the theories and basics of the long sword, I hope you have come to understand that using the long sword isn't about beating your adversary to death with a tire iron. Instead, it is a precision cutting tool. You always want to be in control of yourself by following the path, perfecting your guards and maintaining a proper stance. If you do so, you will be successful in attacking your adversary.

Michael Jordan once said, "You have to monitor your fundamentals constantly because the only thing that changes will be your attention to them. The fundamentals will never change." I encourage you to read this book more than once to cement these principles into your practice. I also recommend that you seek out sword instructors and groups to put these principles into action. The only way to really make these concepts second nature is to practice with other people. Because your safety is your responsibility, you should take this challenge seriously.

To close, I want to leave you with the wisdom of Joseph Swetnam, the 17th century author of *The School of the Noble and Worthy Science of Defence*:

"A fair tongue is more necessary for a valorous man [...] and shall more prevail than your Sword, or any other weapon whatsoever. A faire tongue is as a precious balm to bear about you although it is not sufficient to heal wounds, yet it may be a preventative to keep you without hurts."

I salute you for your interest my friend! Stay on the path, be safe in your journey, and I hope your study of the sword helps you grow as a human being.

Finis

Appendix A:
Outfitting for the Journey

Safety is paramount when you practice with a sword, and it is maintained with the proper protective gear. Before buying any gear, talk to a professional sword fighting instructor or group. Do your research.

Head and Face Protection

You must wear full head and face protection during any sword drill involving another person. The two most common forms of protection for the head are a fencing mask, like those used in the Olympics, and a metal helmet. Even though the fencer's helmet will give you the minimum protection needed for practicing with the long sword, it was never designed to handle the repeated concussive blow or thrusts you will practice. There is also no protection for the back of the head, although sometimes sword fighters will add a flap of hard leather or a knee pad to it.

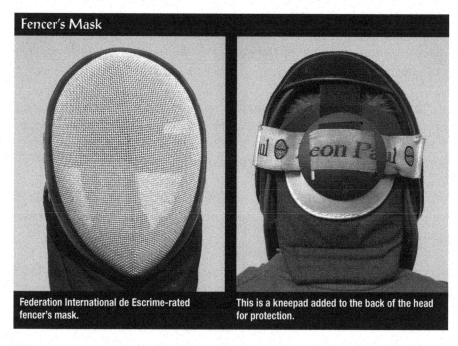

Fencer's Mask

Federation International de Escrime-rated fencer's mask.

This is a kneepad added to the back of the head for protection.

You can easily find fencing helmets at fencing stores online. FIE-rated masks can cost anywhere from $100 to $180. Never buy a secondhand fencing mask. Your face and your eyes are worth the investment. Fencing masks weaken over time and must be replaced regularly. The grill of the fencing mask should regularly be tested with a device called a "punch test" every six months and before every competition. Any mask with rust on the grill should NEVER be used. Olympic fencers have died in competition when the face grill was pierced by their opponent's sword.

The metal helmet comes in a variety of styles. Be certain that yours has a full-face grill. The grill should be "tight" enough that your training partner's blade never slips through. You want your metal helmet to be at least 18-gauge steel but not thicker than 14 gauge. Anything thinner than 18 gauge will not withstand the blows from a long sword, while if you exceed 14 gauge, your helmet will be too heavy for you to wear. Even though they are made of metal, 18 gauge helmets aren't meant to take strong, repeated strikes. Instead, use them for light training.

Good quality metal helmets can be expensive. Also, it is best if you have one made to your measurements for a proper fit. A custom-made metal helmet can take quite some time to make depending on the style you choose.

Throat Protection

Under your helmet or mask, you must wear a *gorget* (gor-jet) to protect your throat. Gorget is French for "throat." There are different types of gorgets, and you need to decide which type you prefer. You can find them made out of leather, metal or a combination of the two, which is known as brigandine. You will need a gorget that fits around your neck without being so tight that it restricts your breathing or so loose that it

Leather Gorget

The heavy leather gorget offers lightweight protection for your trachea.

allows throat to be hit. I also suggest you purchase a gorget that extends over your collarbones for added protection against head and shoulder attacks.

Metal Gorget

This metal gorget covers your trachea and cervical spine but leaves your shoulders unprotected.

Brigandine Gorgets

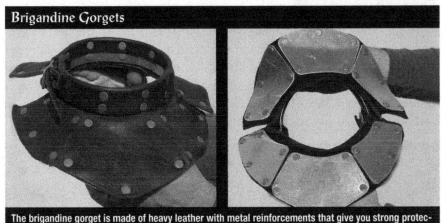

The brigandine gorget is made of heavy leather with metal reinforcements that give you strong protection over your throat and shoulders.

Protective Clothing

There are a variety of choices when it comes to protecting your arms and torso. These choices include simple ready-to-wear modern fencing jackets, historical garb such as gambesons, and custom suits of armor.

The modern fencing jacket is the minimum safety requirement for your body. I recommend choosing a modern fencing jacket made out of leather or a canvas-type material. FIE-rated fencing jackets are designed to stop a broken modern fencing blade from impaling the body, but they still offer little protection from hard thrusts or cuts in regular sword drills. It's a good idea to combine your jacket with a plastic plastron to protect your chest and upper abdomen. Prices tend to run between $50 and $200 for jackets. The plastron usually is $25 to $50.

Modern Fencing Jacket

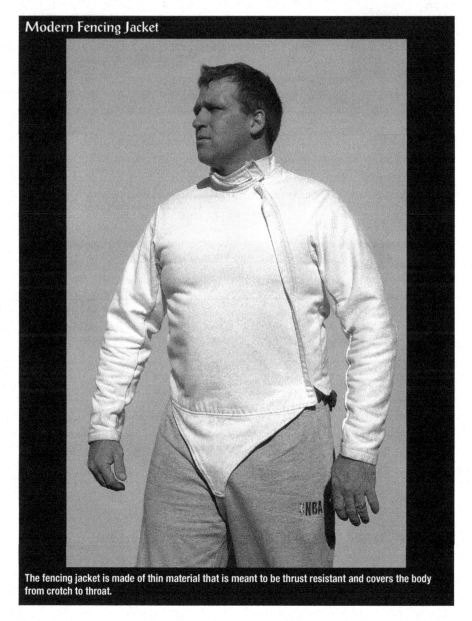

The fencing jacket is made of thin material that is meant to be thrust resistant and covers the body from crotch to throat.

Plastron

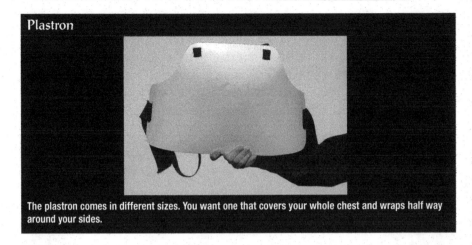

The plastron comes in different sizes. You want one that covers your whole chest and wraps half way around your sides.

The gambeson is a heavily padded jacket that was used in the 15th and 16th centuries. Knights wore these under their armor and chain mail for protection and comfort. It has a more historical look and feel than the fencing jacket, which some contemporary students and instructors prefer. You can find gambesons from suppliers like Chivalry Sports, Museum

Gambeson

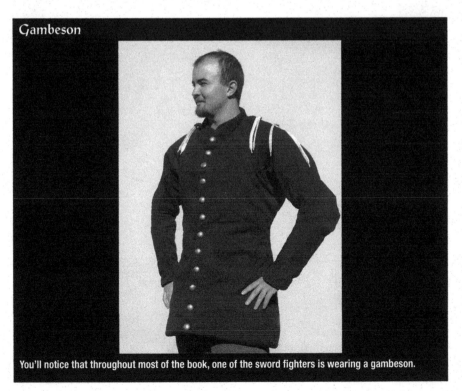

You'll notice that throughout most of the book, one of the sword fighters is wearing a gambeson.

Replicas or Revival Clothing. You can add field hockey pads and children's shin guards to protect your arm and leg joints. While the gambeson is better padded than a modern-fencing jacket, it is still only a cloth buffer between you and your training partner's swords.

By far the most expensive and beautiful piece of body protection you can own is also the most historically accurate. Unlike the jacket or gambeson, a suit of armor takes a lot of time to be custom fit to your body. You want it to allow freedom of movement while providing the proper protection. Poorly fitted armor can injure you or impede your movement. Armor is held in place by leather straps that should already be installed. If they're not, you need to do it. Without the straps, you have the equivalent of a very expensive metal pile.

Suit of Armor

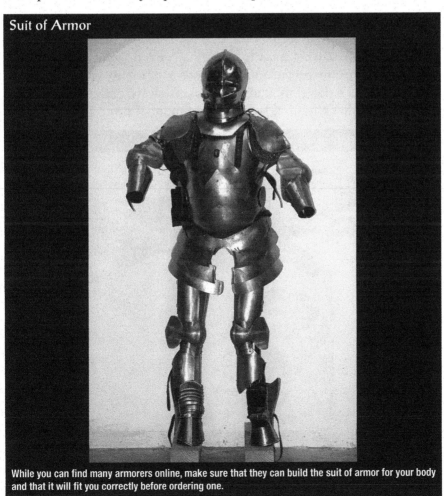

While you can find many armorers online, make sure that they can build the suit of armor for your body and that it will fit you correctly before ordering one.

To protect your legs, wear leggings. Look for a pair of pants made out of stout material such as canvas or jean. Look for leggings with double layers of wool or else consider wearing modern-fencing knickers. You may wish to wear a pair of shin guards for added protection if you're not wearing full armor. No exposed skin should be visible during practice. Shorts with shin guards are not acceptable.

Hand and Wrist Protection

As you learned in the book, your hands are protected by the quillons, but that doesn't mean they are always safe. For hand and wrist protection, consider leather gauntlets, hockey or lacrosse gloves or steel gauntlets.

You can purchase leather gloves at fencing supply stores, motorcycle shops or on the Internet. Unless you know your glove size, try a few on for proper fit before ordering online. It is important that the cuff of the glove extends past your wrist to about halfway up your forearm. Long cuffs are important because they prevent a thrust to your wrist from slipping between the glove and your jacket's sleeve and into your flesh. Unpadded leather gauntlets offer the minimum of protection.

Leather Gauntlets

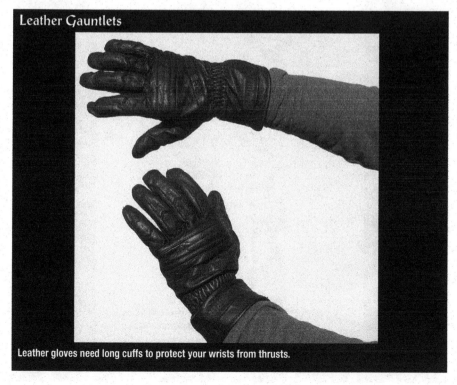

Leather gloves need long cuffs to protect your wrists from thrusts.

Hockey gloves offer excellent padded protection for your hands from the concussive force of a sword strike. I have found that lacrosse gloves offer better hand and wrist mobility with just slightly less padding than hockey gloves. Be aware that hockey gloves and lacrosse gloves will affect your maneuverability and sword grip.

Hockey Gloves or Lacrosse Gloves

Hockey and lacrosse gloves are a modern day equivalent of medieval armor gauntlets.

Steel gauntlets, when fitted properly, will protect your hands fully while allowing proper grip and movement of the sword. There are two types: mitten gauntlets and finger gauntlets. Mitten gauntlets have pieces of metal that cover the whole hand. Finger gauntlets have many pieces of metal that cover each finger; they are generally more attractive than mitten gauntlets but don't offer as much protection. If your hands get hit by the sword when wearing finger gauntlets, the force of the strike is transferred to the finger bone located directly below the piece that was hit. If you are wearing mitten gauntlets and take that same hit to your fingers, the force of the blow is transferred over the whole hand, much like a bullet proof vest transfers the force of a shot to the whole torso. Like the steel helmet, you need to be aware of the thickness of the metal the gauntlets are made of. You will want to purchase gauntlets that are 18-gauge minimum and no thicker than 14-gauge metal. The 18-gauge gauntlets are the low end of protection for your hands and may not be enough to protect your hands and fingers. The steel gauntlets are more expensive compared with the other choices.

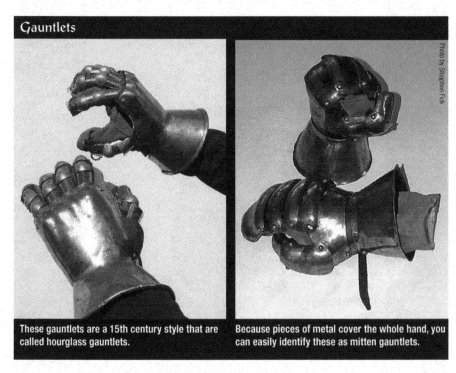

Gauntlets

Photo by Sheaghan Fick

These gauntlets are a 15th century style that are called hourglass gauntlets.

Because pieces of metal cover the whole hand, you can easily identify these as mitten gauntlets.

No matter how much protection your wear, there is no guarantee that you will not be bruised or injured if struck. As my wife says to me all too frequently: "Move faster, block better. The best strategy is to not be hit."

She is a fountain of wisdom.

Appendix B:
The Sword—Pretty vs. Practical

There are many long swords out there of varying quality, styles and prices. You may practice with whatever kind of sword you wish. You can get swords made out of metal, wood, fiberglass or plastic. If you are purchasing a metal long sword, it must have the following properties:

The blade should be made of tempered steel and not stainless steel. Preferably the tempered steel should not be above 55 on the Rockwell hardness scale. This allows the blade to be strong and rigid enough to strike and defend with, yet flexible enough to bend rather than shatter if it's hit on the flat. Stainless steel has some alloys that create the stainless attributes but also decreases the swords strength and toughness.

Cable TV has shows that offer dozens of swords and knives at ridiculous prices. These swords and knives are almost always made of stainless steel. While stainless steel is pretty and you never have to worry about rust, the metal is too brittle for contact. If you swing two stainless steel swords against each other, there's very good chance they'll shatter. This could result in tiny shards of steel flying through the air, which can both injure onlookers and penetrate your fencing mask's grill, causing serious injury to your eyes.

Your practice sword must be rebated, which means dull. NEVER use a sharp sword for practicing. Not only do you run the risk of injury to

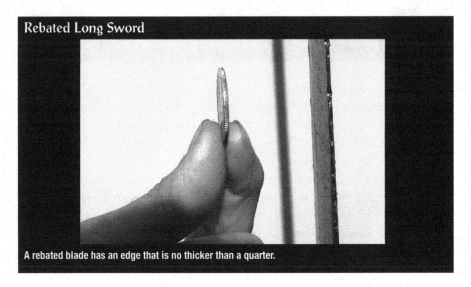

Rebated Long Sword

A rebated blade has an edge that is no thicker than a quarter.

your training partners, but also you can just as easily injure yourself. Unless you are practicing cutting or thrusting against targets such as rolled mats, water bottles, cardboard tubes, a sharp sword is unacceptable. Many swords can be ordered rebated from the manufacturer. If you look at the edge of a properly rebated sword you will see that it is about the thickness of the edge of a quarter. If you do have a sword that has an edge, you will need to remove that edge before you use it for your practice. Never use a grinder on your blade or you run the risk of destroying its temper. The sharp point of the sword must be rounded down to at least the diameter of dime. This helps prevent the sword from penetrating protective garments.

Rounded Point

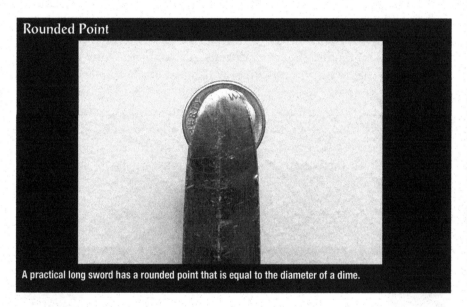

A practical long sword has a rounded point that is equal to the diameter of a dime.

Wood swords, commonly known as wooden wasters, are historically accurate to practice with. The advantage is that they are far less expensive and more forgiving to the new student. Choose a wooden sword designed for serious contact that will not easily splinter. Some of the best kinds of wooden wasters are made of hickory or ash. Oak will splinter relatively quickly so do not use oak in your practice. Some waster manufacturers are New Stirling Arms and Purpleheart Armory. Certain techniques will feel different when done with wooden blades rather than steel blades. It is important, however, that you use wood against wood and steel against steel. Otherwise, the drills will not work properly. You will also damage the wooden swords if they are not used against other wooden swords.

Some manufacturers also produce aluminum swords. These swords give you the feel of steel swords without the weight. These swords are made with thicker metal than steel swords and are still lighter. If you use an aluminum sword, you can only use it with another aluminum sword. If you use it against a steel sword, it will get nicked, exposing sharp edges around the nicks. This is dangerous to you and your partner.

There are also design aspects that your sword must have to perform the various drills properly:

Quillons: The cross guards between the hilt and the sword blade. They can be curved, straight or S-shaped. The edges of the blade must match the direction of the quillons. Any quillons in the shape of lightning bolts, crossbones or other sharp objects should be avoided if you intend to use it. The quillons must also not be angled towards the hands, because that style can injure your hands or wrist.

Sword Length: Sword length is a personal matter. The length of your sword is dictated by your height. The quillons should not be above your naval with the point on the ground. Another measurement is that the pommel should not go above the base of your sternum. If you get a sword that is too long, you can lose the ability to control it.

Sword Weight: Your sword should not weigh more than 3.5 to 4 pounds. Anything above this weight will be too heavy for you to use safely and is not historically accurate. Swords did not weigh 14 pounds. They feel heavy when you start your training but that is because you must develop the muscles necessary to control the sword. If you have a sword that is too heavy, the weight of the sword will make it difficult for you to control its momentum along the path. Also, by trying to use an unrealistically heavy sword, you can pull or strain a muscle.

Remember, there is no such thing as a "safe sword." While you have removed the edge and the point of your sword, it is still a large piece of metal or wood. The mass alone is enough to cause damage, so it is up to you to keep safety a priority at all times. When starting your studies and purchasing a sword, get a sword that is not too heavy to control or too light to defend yourself against other swords. A wooden sword is a good long sword to start with. However, ultimately you are the only one that can keep your sword from hurting someone.

Appendix C:
Sword Movies

While there are thousands of movies that have sword fighting in them, I've stuck to movies made specifically for Western audiences. I can't promise that all of them are "good," but they do have fun action scenes in them. I've broken them up into categories and listed the actor who plays the main swordsman. When watching movies, remember that the idea behind a fight in the movie is to tell a story. It has to be big enough that it can be seen and show the intentions of the actors. During a real sword fight, however, the goal is to go home safe. It is difficult to put a technically accurate fight in a movie, and there are some that do better than others.

Movies With Long Swords

Conan the Barbarian with Arnold Schwarzenegger
This is one of the movies that got me started in sword fighting. It's a classic!

A Knight's Tale with Heath Ledger
This movie has a fun mix of knightly tournaments and disco music. As long as you aren't expecting historical accuracy, this is a fun movie. I don't know how accurate they were, but part of the rationale behind tournaments was showing off for all the spectators.

The Chronicles of Narnia: The Lion, The Witch and the Wardrobe
with William Moseley
In the final battle of the movie, there are a lot of different kinds of weapons, but you'll be able to notice that all the cuts are from the shoulder.

The Chronicles of Narnia: Prince Caspian with William Moseley
The final duel between our hero Peter and the villain King Miraz is a very good sword-and-shield fight. Also, the bad guys have the coolest helmets I've seen in movies in a long time. They are reminiscent of 16th century parade armors.

Kingdom of Heaven with Orlando Bloom
Liam Neeson's character teaches Bloom's character the *posta falcone*! Remember that is the guard from Filippo Vadi's treatise *Arte Gladiatoria*.

The Lord of the Rings Trilogy with Viggo Mortensen
Peter Jackson's trilogy did a great job with sword fighting. Sharp viewers will notice Aragorn use *posta finestra* to *posta falcone* a lot of times in all three films.

Henry V with Kenneth Branagh
This film version of Shakespeare's play has some sword-and-shield fights that use weapons other than the long sword. The fights are filled with big movements that look powerful but are actually slow because cuts from the shoulder will always move slower than cuts from the elbow.

Movies With Other Swords

Tristan & Isolde with James Franco
There are some good fights in this movie. I especially like the fight around the slave cart because there is a lot of manipulation of balance and movement.

The Duelists with Keith Carradine
This movie has some of the most historically accurate fights with a military saber and small sword. The fights give the viewer real insight into the fear and adrenaline involved in a duel.

Rob Roy with Liam Neeson
This film features a great climatic fight between a basket-hilted broadsword and a rapier.

Scaramouche with Stewart Granger
The climatic sword fight is six minutes long and was shot in a single take. It's the longest single-take sword fight in Hollywood history. This fight was very similar to fights of that era and features Olympic saber-fencing techniques.

The Court Jester with Danny Kaye
This is one of the all-time funniest sword-fighting movies out there. Actors Danny Kaye and Basil Rathbone are both great fencers and put on a tremendous show. The movie features fun sword fights and great tongue twisters plus magnetic armor!

Master and Commander: The Far Side of the World with Russell Crowe
During the ship-to-ship fight scenes, the actors had to use every part of their weapons for defense and offense. You can see this when they fight under the decks in the ship's cramped quarters. The weapons used in this movie are primarily the cutlass and the spadroon.

The Three Musketeers with Michael York
This is another movie that made me want to study fencing and learn more about sword fighting. It has great fights, but the remarks made by secondary characters are by far the most amusing part of the movie.

The Princess Bride with Cary Elwes
This movie has one of the all-time classic rapier fights. While not a technically accurate fight, the fight has become a pop-culture icon. Also, the four fencing masters that our heroes Westley and Inigo discuss—Ridolfo Capo Ferro, Camillo Agrippa, Rocco Bonetti and Girard Thibault—lived during the 16th and 17th centuries. They all wrote treatises, except for Bonetti, that are still available today.

Non-Sword Movies With Sword Fights

Hellboy II: The Golden Army with Ron Perlman
This film has a very good sword fight at the end between Hellboy and the villainous Prince Nuada.

Indiana Jones and the Kingdom of the Crystal Skull with Harrison Ford
There is a fun sword fight between two characters who are on the back of different vehicles, speeding through a jungle in South America. Talk about balance issues!

Glossary of Terms

Basic Parry: The basic parry is a defensive movement that with practice becomes second nature. It can take two forms: the "V" and the "A." The "V" is the natural movement while the "A" is a trained movement and the stronger of the two.

Center Line: The ideal line of attack is the center line. You always want to attack your adversary on your center line, and he always wants to position you in his center line.

Circle Step: The circle step changes your angle but maintains the measure, so you never more closer or farther away from your adversary. Like the diameter of a circle, you are always at the same distance.

Contracted Guards: These guards start close to your body, so you need to extend your arms out when you transition.

Dui Tempe: In *dui tempe*, you defend the attack then counterattack.

Extended Guards: These guards don't start close to the body. Instead, you need to contract the sword and then extend it with your arms to deliver a cut.

False Edge: The false edge, sometimes known as the "back edge" or "short edge," is the part of the blade that faces your body and does not face your adversary. The false edge is always the edge closest to the webbing of the thumbs.

Feint: When you feint, you perform an attack that you expect your adversary to defend against. However, you plan to change your center line suddenly.

Fendente: The *fendente* is a descending cut that moves from the high line to the low line. It can be cut from the shoulder, elbow or wrist. If you cut from your left side, it is called a *fendente sinestra*. The trajectory is down from eye to knee.

Foible: The foible is the last third of the blade and is the farthest part from the hilt. It is the fastest part of the blade.

Forte: The forte comprises the first third of the blade, starting from the *quillons*. It is the best defense for a swordsman because it is the strongest part of the blade.

Guards: Sword guards, or wards, are positions you change and assume in the midst of a fight. There are three categories discussed in this book: high, middle and low guards. The guards can also be broken into extended and contracted guards.

Handle: The handle is the section between the pommel and the *quillons*.

High Guards: The high guards are guards that don't necessarily close a line, but they are at shoulder level or above. There are four high guards, which correspond to the four sides of your head: the front, back, right and left side. They are the *posta finestra, posta di donna, posta di donna sinestra* and *pulsativa*.

High Line: The area above your waist is the high line.

Hilt: The hilt includes the pommel, the *quillons* and the handle.

Inside Line: The imaginary line that you would draw from your weapon hand to your opposite shoulder along the inside of the weapon arm is the inside line.

Lines of Attack: Lines of attack are the lines you use to launch an attack at your adversary.

Lines of the Body: Lines of the body are lines that you want to defend. They also tell you when a line is open and where the attack will come from. They consist of the outside, inside, high and low line.

Long Sword: The long sword was used between the 14th and 16th centuries and is most commonly associated with knights. It is also known as the hand-and-a-half sword, great sword or bastard sword.

Low Guards: The low guards close your low line so your sword is always pointed at the ground. The low guards are the *denti di cinghiale, tutta porta di ferro, mezza porta di ferro* and *coda lunga*.

Low Line: The area below your waist is the low line.

Measure: Measure refers to the distance between two adversaries.

Mezza: The *mezza* refers to the middle third of the blade.

Mezzana: The *mezzana* is an ascending and descending cut that always ends in middle guard.

Mezzo Tempo: In *mezzo* tempo, you attack before your adversary completes his attack.

Middle Guards: The middle guards close your high line from your waist to your shoulders and always place your sword between you and your adversary. The middle guards are the *posta breve, posta lunga, posta corona* and *posta de bicornio*.

Outside Line: The imaginary line that starts at your weapon hand and runs along the outside of that arm to your shoulder is the outside line.

Pommel: The pommel is the counterweight at the end of the sword handle, and it helps balance the weight of the blade, making it easier to use and move around.

Pulling the Hilt: Pulling the hilt refers to when you strike at an adversary and pull the blade back. More to the point, you perform a slice by pulling your hilt with your hands.

Quillons: The purpose of the *quillons* is to protect your hands from a downward cut and separate the blade from the handle. They are also referred to as the "cross guard."

Rapier: The rapier is a single-handed, double-edged, long thrusting sword used from the late 16th century through the end of the 17th century.

Side Sword: The side sword was popular in the 16th century and is a cross between the long sword and rapier.

Slope Step: The slope step is a forward right or forward left step that closes measure on a new center line. When you slope step, move the foot that corresponds to the direction you are moving; that foot also becomes or maintains the lead position.

Sotani: The *sotani* is an ascending blow that can be cut from the shoulder, elbow or wrist. It moves from a low line to a high line. If you cut from the left side, it is called the *sotani sinestra*. The trajectory is up from the knee and out the eye.

Stesso Tempo: In *stesso* tempo, you defend at the same time that you attack.

Sweet Spot: The sweet spot is the best place on your sword to cut your adversary with. You may hear it also called the "center of percussion."

Tempo: Tempo refers to timing. When you are facing your adversary, the time that you keep is how long a particular move, step or action takes.

The Path: The path is the way that your sword and arm will move around you from guard to guard smoothly.

Thrust: The thrust— which is called the *punte* in Italian—is a transition from a contracted guard to an extended guard on linear path.

Traverse Step: The traverse step is when you step out of your adversary's line of attack to the left or right side. When you traverse, you actually widen the distance between you and him.

True Edge: The edge facing away from your body and toward your adversary is known as the true edge. It's also sometimes referred to as the "long edge."

About the Author

Steaphen Fick is the founder of the Davenriche European Martial Artes School as well as the International Medieval Tournament Association, two organizations dedicated to bringing medieval combat styles to the 21st century. With 20 years of experience in European martial arts, Fick is an internationally ranked provost and two-time rapier winner at the International Sword and Martial Arts Convention. He has also competed in fully armored tournaments and has taught in the United States, England and Canada. He currently resides in Santa Clara, California.